Truths of Illusion

Belangela G. Tarazona

Copyrights

This is a work of fiction. All names, characters and incidents of this publication other than those clearly in the public domain are fictitious and any resemblance to real persons, living or dead, is purely coincidental.

No part of this publication may be reproduced, stored in a retrieval system or transmitted, in any form or by any means, without the prior permission in writing of the author, nor be otherwise circulated in any form of binding or cover other than in which it is published and without a similar condition including this condition being imposed on the subsequent purchaser.

Cover: Amedeo Bodigliani (1884-1920), Alice (1918). Kindly made available by Statens Museum for Kunst www.smk.dk

Copyright © Belangela G. Tarazona 2014
www.bg-tarazona.net
ISBN: 978-8799737901

Content

At the Confessional And 1

What No One Knew Of The Dead Man 38

Presumed Indecent: The Story Of Maruja Colina 80

About the Author 119

At the Confessional And Other Calamities

"Father, I've sinned."

"Confess, my daughter."

I rushed to confess, the words piling up in my mouth for fear of forgetting something.

"I stole mangoes, I didn't do my homework and I stepped on Nazaret's packed lunch."

"By stealing, you violated the seventh commandment of God's law!" said the priest. "Not doing your homework isn't a sin, that's just plain laziness. And about stepping on the food…do you know how many people in the world are starving?"

"Father, it's her own fault for tossing my bag into the trashcan," I replied.

I kept my head bowed, the black strands of my bangs covering my eyes.

"Dear, there's no ill will between good Christians and I can see you are too young to hold a grudge," the priest explained. "To reach perfection, read Matthew 29 and say three Lord's Prayers, with repentance.

Heartfelt, you know? Otherwise don't take communion."

I frowned.

"Matthew 29?" I asked. "You mean Matthew 19, right?"

"I mean Matthew 29! Go with God, my daughter!" he snapped.

"Amen, Father."

I rushed back to the pew and knelt next to where grandma was sitting. I recited the Lord's Prayer.

> *Our Father, which art in heaven,*
> *Hallowed be thy Name.*
> *Thy Kingdom come.*
> *Thy will be done on earth,*
> *As it is in heaven...*

"Caridad I hope you didn't forget any of your sins, did you?" whispered Granny Piedad.

"No, I didn't, granny. I told him everything."

**

Sunday - a week earlier

I sensed that my mother was up to something by the way she came into our bedroom. I was playing with Magdalena, my 8-year-old sister, and some plastic dolls we had received as a Christmas present, years ago. We were pretending we were at school, sitting on the floor with open books. Magdalena and I were the teachers and the dolls were the students. Mom just stood there, silently, looking around at first, and then she went over to the night table beside Magdalena's bed.

My sister and I looked at her, a little bit surprised, and waited for whatever she had to say, but she did not utter a word, at first. Instead, she wandered a bit further away from us.

"What are you two playing at?" Mom asked at last.

"We are playing at being the teacher!" said Magdalena.

Mom nodded at the doll Magdalena was holding up in explanation.

"Caridad, we have had to send Dolores out of town," my mother began. "You know, to spend some time with Granny Mildred. The problem is, now, we need someone to take Granny Piedad to Mass on Sundays. We think you would be just perfect to do that. What do you think? You'll get five cents to buy whatever you want."

"Is Granny Mildred ill?" I asked, worried.

"No, no, it's just that she needs some company," my mother replied. "So Dolores has agreed to stay with her for a while.

Anyway, if you go to Mass with Granny Piedad you can also help her to carry the shopping bags afterwards."

"Yes, of course I'd love to be Granny Piedad's companion!" I said, smiling.

"Thanks for helping out Caridad," said my mom. "Then we're all set. Next Sunday, you'll be the one who goes to church with Granny Piedad!"

Mom paused before leaving the room and turned back to us.

"By the way, you have to confess your sins," she explained. "Is that ok?"

Dolores had told me something about that before, but I couldn't remember what it was.

"Yes, yes, I guess so," I said, looking at the floor.

"You can always ask the priest if you don't know how to do it," mom reassured me.

Then she knocked at the door twice and left, leaving behind the breeze of rose and narcissus from her "Je Reviens" perfume.

**

"Congratulations, sis!" said Magdalena. "That's a big deal, don't you think?"

She shook my arm and gave me a big smile.

"Now you're the one who accompanies

Granny Piedad to church!" she continued. "What an honor! Dolores told me that if someone is given responsibilities, it's because they are becoming mature! I'm proud of you, sis!"

Her little face shone proudly like the sun.

"Thanks Magdalena, I don't know," I wondered. "I thought you only became mature when you got your very first period. Dolores told me that once."

I tried to not make a big deal of it.

"Your period?"

"You know, when girls bleed every month," I shrugged. "I thought you knew about it."

"When does that happen?"

"I don't know, it comes when it comes, I guess."

Magdalena looked at the doll she was holding and then asked:

"Shall we go to bed? We have to get up early tomorrow."

"Yeah, I think you're right! We'd better stop playing for now, but before we go to bed, we have to tidy up this room!" I said.

I tickled her and we began to pick up the toys.

**

Dolores used to hum songs of the Christian chorus wherever she went. She also helped the Charity Group raising money, and mom gave her permission to become a member of the church choir. The truth is that I didn't have even half of her credentials, but here I was, presented with the offer that also meant a step up in the family hierarchy. Why did she give it up so quickly? I'd assumed someone had to take care of Granny Mildred, but she wasn't ill, was she? I pondered over these questions while trying to fall asleep.

I felt flattered by the huge responsibility laid upon me, but it was also frightening. I only read the Holy Bible, because I saw it as a book of tales, just like the Aeneid, Nibelung, Don Quixote or Ivanhoe.

To open each of these books was like being sucked into another world. Actually, it was like a static journey to other places that I dreamed of visiting one day. As soon as I finished one book, I grabbed the next. The more I read, the more I craved the next book. Sometimes, I did not even understand the real meaning of them. I understood the essence of those treasures many years later, but at the time, the thrill of reading them was all I needed. The books had changed the way I spoke to the point that my classmates made fun of me.

"Piedad, why do you speak like that?" Nazaret had once asked me. "You sound like an old lady!"

Her two lapdogs, Thea Ziegler and Daniela Franco, had nodded and repeated every single word Nazaret spewed. The bully had drilled into me with her eyes, tightening her lips so much that no laugh could escape her orc's mouth. My sister's voice brought me back to the present.

"Caridad! Caridad! Imagine all the sweets you can buy with five cents a week!" Magdalena whispered in the darkness of our bedroom.

"You know what? The first thing I'll buy is a cool soft drink," I told her.

"Which flavor? No, don't tell me: Grape, I bet."

"Grape, of course, it has to be grape," I agreed. "Pity that I won't be able to share it with you."

I sighed and pulled the sheets up to my chin.

"Never mind sis, one day," Magdalena whispered.

"Yes, sweetie. One day," I whispered back.

"Good night, sis."

My mind wandered while trying to fall asleep. I thought of Nazaret, my mom, grape soda...and Dolores.

**

With a towel draped over her shoulders, Granny Piedad went to take a shower.

She put a few drops of Jean Naté perfume behind her ears. After all, she was having an appointment with God. It was Sunday. It was time to go to church. Therefore, Granny Piedad thought she should look and smell her best. She slipped her arms through her dress like she was putting on a T-shirt. When she was done dressing, she scooped up a small amount of Brylcreem from a jar, rubbed her fingers together, and brushed her long hair back. To finish, she twisted its length a couple of times to make a chignon.

"Caridad, I'd love to see you wearing your long-sleeved red turtleneck pullover and your green skirt with the small prints," said Granny Piedad. "Would you?"

She knew I would. Granny Piedad had a smarmy tone that had a way of making make me do what I was told.

The skirt was made of polyester and was way too short for my bird-like legs. In fact, it actually made me look like a heron. I was at risk of bumping into my classmates at church and the last thing in the world I wanted was for them to see me wearing the horrid thing my granny called a skirt.

What if I bumped into Nazaret? I thought.

That orc was my tormentor at school; I didn't want to imagine the mocking I'd receive if she got to see me wearing those ugly clothes. The trendy clothes to wear were jeans and cotton blouses, not polyester and turtlenecks. I would have to fly to the moon to avoid ridicule, but try explaining that to Granny Piedad. We were going to God's house, so no expense was spared. If granny wanted it, I had to wear the things.

"I look like a God damned elf in this outfit!" I whispered to the mirror.

"Hurry up Caridad! We haven't got all day," Granny Piedad called to me. "Remember that I don't walk that fast. Have you made a list of your sins?"

"Yeees, granny, you want to hear them?" I asked her, while braiding my pigtails.

"No, no, no, just leave it to the priest."

It was not even 8 o'clock, but I could feel the wave of heat that blew into the house when we opened the door. I could see it was a deep blue, cloudless morning; which was unusual in the Town of the Mist. It seemed as if the sea had agreed to swap places with the sky. I could not help looking at myself from top to toe and imagining myself leaving the church at 12 o'clock in the outfit I was wearing; the noon sun
would be unforgiving.

**

The town church sits on one side of the

main square. The bell tower and the parish house flank the main building, to the right. The red brick dome can be seen on the left-hand side, and this is topped with a spire-shaped cross. Along the side of the dome are rows of palms trees, which contrast with the white walls. Three massive mahogany doors provide an entrance to the nave of the church.

My grandmother likes to sit on the right side of the nave leading to the aisle, because, as she puts it: "It is near the confessional and the departure hall, just in case you have to leave Mass early."

"Father, I have sinned," I began.

"Confess my daughter."

"I ate the icing off a cake my granny was looking after."

"A cake Granny Piedad was looking after...." The priest wondered. "Why?"

"Yes, it was Chepo's birthday," I explained. "He is my neighbor's husband. His wife was holding a surprise party for him, and she didn't want him to suspect she was up to something, so she asked Granny Piedad to keep the cake at home in the meantime. I couldn't help it. It was this moist chocolate pound cake, with chocolate fudge frosting."

I paused and looked into the window of the confessional, through which you can see the priest.

"Continue, my daughter."

"It all started with a simple touch at the

bottom, then I guess I worked all the way up to the top, but I didn't eat any more of the cake than that."

"What happened next?"

"Granny and mom were furious," I said. "It was embarrassing having to explain my actions to our neighbor, but she took it well, and you know what? She sent a nice piece of cake to us! Of course, granny made sure that I didn't get a single piece, saying that I'd had enough already. What a nerve, don't you think, Father?"

"Say three Lord's Prayers, I have to leave," the priest confessed. "The Mass is about to start."

"Amen, Father."

We could hear the voices of the church choir singing in the background:

Te presentamos el vino y el pan, bendito seas por siempre Señor...

The priest dedicated the Mass to those who had died in town in the last month. At the end, he said solemnly: "You can go home in peace".

Granny Piedad and I were on our way to the exit, when some ladies who called themselves members of the Legion of

Mary stopped her to chat. Judging by the snatches of conversation I overheard, they were talking about a woman who had ran off with another member of the church, leaving her husband and children behind without a trace.

Bored of the "pious" character of the conversation, I walked away from the women a little to look at the reliefs on the walls, which depicted various scenes from the life of Jesus. At 12 o'clock, the church bells rang, signifying that the time of worship was over, and we headed home.

My neck was itching because of the heat, but as we approached the cemetery we popped into Tito's little grocery shop. He was there, wrapping a bunch of white carnations that an old lady had purchased to lay on someone's grave. The old lady paid for the flowers and left in the direction of the cemetery.

"Why are they in there?"

I pointed to a pair of brown shoes inside one of the little bottle fridges.

"That fridge doesn't work anymore, so I use it to showcase goods," Tito shrugged. "See, I also have shoe polish, razors, and cotton yarn."

He gestured to the items by making a circular movement with his arm. I smiled and kept looking around. The little shop had three bottle fridges arranged in a "U" shape, as if protecting Tito from the visitors and urging them to come no further. On the back wall were two shelves displaying bottles with red tags that read "Cacique", and underneath the shelves was a cabinet full of trinkets, nail polish, and old yellowed, magazines.

I kept checking the place out until Granny Piedad dragged me back to reality. She put five one-cent coins into my palm.

"They're yours," granny said. "Buy what you want."

"Thanks granny!" I exclaimed.

I alternately looked down at the coins in my palm and back up at her. I closed my fingers to feel my hard-earned money. When I opened my eyes, Tito and Granny Piedad were smiling at me.

"May I have a cool soft drink, please?"

"Which flavor?" asked Tito, regally.

"Grape, please."

I handed him a cent.

Both he and granny laughed in unison.

"What?"

"The soft drink costs five cents," he said, almost apologetically.

My jaw dropped.

I inwardly moaned that I had just earned the money and now I had to hand it all to Tito. But I did want that grape soda, so I begrudgingly gave him the remaining four coins and he opened the bottle for me.

**

We thanked our Lord for everything, especially before breakfast, when the day started. Then granny served bollos, which were balls of precooked maize flour dough, boiled, and served with melted butter. While she was sprinkling grated white cheese over them, she started nagging me about my sins.

"You must not forget your sins! Keep your list up-to-date. I don't want you to forget anything!"

She pestered me without even taking her eyes off the dishes she was preparing for breakfast.

"I know, granny."

I could hear "Martín Valiente", the radio drama broadcast by Radio Rumbos.

Magdalena and Gustavo joined Granny Piedad and jokingly reminded me about the horrible clothes I had to wear to church.

"Keep quiet, I can't hear!" Granny Piedad said, trying to pay attention to what was going on in the radio drama.

Magdalena took my arm.

"What?" I asked her, visibly annoyed by her teasing.

"Dolores' 'small lemons' are popping out."

Magdalena said it with a mischievous smile.

"Where did you hear that? She's not even here," I wondered.

"Mom bought her the cutest set of bras yesterday and uncle Eladio will take them for her, next time he goes visiting Granny

Mildred. I'm sure Dolores will get her period soon. You know, when girls bleed every month. Remember?"

"What are you two whispering about? Eat your breakfast before it gets cold!" said granny.

Magdalena had piqued my curiosity, and, at the first opportunity, I slipped into Dolores' room to see the bras.

According to Magdalena, mom had put the whole bunch in the top drawer of the chest, and. I opened it discover a selection of the cutest things I had ever seen. White, pale yellow, pink, and blue pastel, they were all pleated in the center to divide the breasts and were adorned with ribbons and tiny glass beads. Tiny lacework finished off the edges of each cup.

I fell in love with the white bra, because of its pearly hue.

I lifted it up against the light coming through the window, and then I put it over my chest to imagine how it would look on me. I eventually placed it back in the drawer, but I could not stop looking at it.

"Stop it Caridad! They will notice!" I said to myself, totally embarrassed by the idea that had flashed across my mind of keeping the white bra for myself.

I took it again and ran to the bathroom. After checking that the coast was clear, I proceeded to put the bra on after almost tearing off the sweater and t-shirt I was wearing.

I put it on in the same way that I'd seen my mother do it. I tried to look at myself in the mirror, but all I could see was my face and collarbones. I had to stand on the edge of the toilet bowl and lean one knee over the sink to see the rest.

It did not look good because the cup of the bra wrinkled right in the center of my chest. I began to mimic Dolores. To give the entire performance more realism, I grabbed some toilet paper, and shoved a piece inside each cup.

Much better, I thought.

I heard footsteps, as if someone was approaching, so I hurriedly put my t-shirt and sweater back on. However, I did not have time to remove the toilet paper still filling out my chest under the bra.

I could feel Granny Piedad's eyes over my shoulder. She could sense something was going on, even though she was unaware of precisely what it was. I could tell by the way she was looking at me, so I spent the rest of the day avoiding her.

"Dinner is served!" Granny Piedad announced.

When we were all sitting around the table, she approached me. Her piercing eyes were like X-rays, and I got the sensation she was seeing right through me, trying to find out what was hiding beneath my sweater. Suddenly, she grabbed its collar in her hand, which felt like a claw, and went directly to my chest to remove whatever was filling it out.

"Look at this!" cried Granny Piedad.

She held up the bunch of toilet paper, as if it was a piece of evidence in a courtroom.

"Are you wearing Dolores' bra?" asked Magdalena.

Gustavo laughed hysterically and my jaw hit the floor."

"Make sure you confess this to the priest!" said Granny Piedad, bursting out laughing, too.

I did not answer and could not finish my meal after this sheer humiliation. I took the dish and left it in the sink.

"Caridad, if you don't want me to tell anyone about this at school, you'll have to iron all my shirts!" called Gustavo.

**

My friend Eva was sitting next to me during one of our breaks at school. I nudged her.

"I got an electric ball!"

Nazaret, who seemed to have ears everywhere, jumped in.

"Yes, and I suppose it starts to jump when you plug it in the socket!" She sneered, hands on hips.

Daniela Franco and Thea Ziegler, her two lapdogs, were laughing and nodding behind her as she approached us.

"It not only jumps, it also blinks when it bounces!" I said, defiantly.

"And you expect us to believe that? Why don't you bring it to school tomorrow so we can have a look at it?"

"I will! By the way, I will also bring a picture of me and my cousin Nadia Comaneci," I insisted.

Eva pulled me away from the group and took me to the restroom. We waited until there was no one else there except for the two of us.

"Are you out of your mind?" Eva wondered. "You don't have an electric ball, do you?"

"Of course not!" I whispered, afraid that somebody could hear us. "I haven't much to tell the priest this Sunday, that's why. It has to be true that I'm lying; otherwise, it won't be a sin. I mean, a real sin, you see? Granny Piedad is driving me crazy with her demand for sins."

"What's a demand?"

"Never mind, Eva. It's no longer fun to go to church, I can tell you. Granny Piedad doesn't let me out of her sight. I can't breathe!"

I was almost sobbing. Eva was

sympathetic, but honest.

"In the meantime, all those bitches are getting onto you!" she warned. "You know what? Pick me up at 7 o'clock tomorrow, we'll think of something!"

"Tomorrow?"

"Yes, tomorrow," Eva insisted. "We can't talk here, can we?"

"Tomorrow is Saturday. You mean Monday, right?"

"Sorry, I forgot it's Friday today!" Eva smiled. "Yes, I mean Monday morning."

"I'll try to leave early enough that Gustavo and Magdalena don't come with us. See you."

"See you then," Eva replied. "I almost forgot. Don't ring the bell! Mom will lose it if you do. It will be 'too early to ring someone's bell', as she puts it."

Eva shook her head, mimicking her mom.

"Just come in through the kitchen door," she added.

"I won't forget. Have a nice weekend."

"You too!"

We heard the school bell ring as we left the restrooms.

**

Maybe I had gone too far in telling people at school about my "Romanian cousin" Nadia Comaneci, never mind the issue of the electric ball, so I had second thoughts about telling the priest at all, but Granny Piedad would not let it go. She was a constant reminder of how accountable we are in the eyes of God.

We talked about my lies during breakfast, lunch, and dinner, but also while braiding my hair, when I came back from school, or just before going to bed.

That Sunday, I went directly to the chapel of forgiveness to get it over with.

The only person in line for confession was a lady close to Granny Piedad's age. She wore a pale pink dress and her hair looked like a ball of cotton candy you get at an amusement park. Her dark eyes were trapped behind a pair of rimmed glasses, and she had a plastic bag tucked under her arm for shopping after Mass.

I approached the line and greeted her by nodding. Words often stuck in my throat when I was in the presence of strangers. I guess the expectation of confessing my sins also made me nervous; to such a degree that I had to wipe my sweaty hands on my skirt.

My turn came and I told the priest everything. Granny Piedad would find out anyway, I was sure. I told him about the ball, and about Nadia Comaneci, and that I hated Nazaret with all my heart.

"You couldn't come up with someone

less well-known?" asked the priest.

I ignored the question about my "cousin" and continued.

"I hate Nazaret, not only for tossing my bag into the trashcan, but for making my days at school a living Hell!"

"Dear, you don't hate her...I'm sure you're confusing anger with hate!"

"What's anger?"

"Anger is the same as being angry, got it?"

"Oh, yes sure, but let me tell you, I don't anger Nazaret," I pointed out. "I hate her. The devil is red- haired and his name is Nazaret."

I heard muffled sounds from the other side of the confessional.

"Father, are you laughing?"

"No, no my daughter," he replied quickly. "Please say three Lord's Prayers. Otherwise, don't take communion!"

**

The dawn was greeted by a silent, but steady, rain that fell tightly and downwards, like a curtain of tiny beads. There was a small pool of water near the window. We had obviously left it open again, although I thought I had closed it before going to bed.

I tiptoed to the bathroom, brushed my teeth, and returned to the bedroom to take my uniform from the chair, where I'd left it the previous night. Once ready, I went down to the kitchen for a glass of milk. The smell of freshly brewed coffee met me at the stairs. My mom was already up, and I found her in the kitchen, reading a newspaper and drinking a cup of coffee.

"Bless me, mom!"

"God bless you," she responded. "Did you sleep well?"

"Yes, I slept tight, and you?"

"Not that well, I had a bit of a headache, but I'm feeling much better now after taking some aspirin."

"Are you getting the flu?"

"I don't know, maybe it's the rain," she shrugged. "You're up early. Aren't you going to wait for Gustavo and Magdalena?"

"I'm meeting up with Eva," I explained. "You know, the Restrepos' only child?"

I pointed to the house on the corner.

"Is she in the same class as you?"

"No, we're in the same grade, but she is in a different class," I said. "We hang out during the breaks."

"Aah, ok."

My mom continued her reading, eyes fixed on the newspaper, never once looking my way.

"Aren't you going to have breakfast?" she asked.

"Only a glass of milk. I promised to pick

Eva up at 7, sharp, and I'm running a bit late."

"Remember your rubber boots and your poncho!" she reminded me. "It will probably rain the whole day."

"Yes, mom. Bless me mother!"

"God bless you!"

I emptied the glass and put it in the sink.

"Wash it!" she said.

I smiled, washed the glass, rinsed it quickly, and placed it on the tabletop to dry. I then left to pick up Eva.

**

I went in through the kitchen door, as Eva had told me to do last Friday. She was still sitting, eating soup for breakfast. She must have nearly finished, because when she saw me, she took the dish and left it in the sink. She shook some crumbs off her chest and washed her hands. Her school bag was lying open on one of the chairs. I could see the Spanish Grammar book we used, a magazine of some sort, showing a man hanging from an apple tree, and something that looked like a pack of cigarettes. From where I was standing, I could read "Derby" on it.

Eva put a hand on my shoulder.

"Let's go!" she said.

"I think I saw a pack of cigarettes in

your bag!" I mentioned, casually.

"I smoke, so what?" she said.

Although she pretended to be angry, her smile betrayed her.

"Do you? That's major! What about your parents?"

"I don't think they'll ever notice," Eva shrugged. "Dad is always drunk and mom is in her own little world."

"When do you smoke?" I wondered. "And how do you hide the smell?"

"Hello? My dad smokes too!" Eva reminded me. "I smoke when they're in their bedroom doing their stuff."

"You mean, making love?"

"Yeah, I heard mom saying the other day that dad's always on her, but he's no use 'cos the booze isn't helping his *stick*, you know?" Eva explained. "Mom said something like, there's more life on the moon than in dad's pants."

"What will you do if they catch you?" I asked, worried.

"I don't know and I don't care," she snapped. "But don't go around sayin' anything. I can trust you on this, right?"

"Of course! We're friends, aren't we?" I replied.

We walked in silence for a while. Eva seemed a bit hurt by my question. The rain was muffling the sounds of the street. Even though the town was shrouded in mist, the cars made waves as they drove through the puddles along the avenue and I began to hum a song.

"Caridad, what are you humming?"

"The song of the Lord of The Horns," I explained. "I mean, Nazaret. You want to hear it?"

"Sure!"

But who is Nazaret?
Nazaret is Belcebú
Belcebú, Belcebú, poor Belcebú
But who is Nazaret?
Nazaret is Belcebú

"Sorry to say so, but that's the most ridiculous thing I've ever heard in my life!" Eva said choking with laughter.

"Who said it should make sense, anyway?" I laughed.

"She bullies you, doesn't she?"

"Yep! She tossed my bag in the trashcan and my lunch disappears," I explained. "She doesn't want anyone to talk to me."

"Why don't you talk to Miss Carlotta about it?" said Eva, pointedly.

"Are you nuts? Miss Carlotta has a soft spot for Nazaret."

"What if Miss Carlotta realizes that Nazaret isn't that special?"

I frowned.

"What do you mean?" I wondered.

"What if I tell you that not everything is how it seems?" Eva said. "Never mind! Forget it!"

I tried to change the subject.

"Eva, why were you eating soup for breakfast?"

"Well, I don't know," she shrugged. "I guess we eat what's there. What about you?"

"We have bollos, arepas, you know, like tortillas filled with cheese and ham." I said. "But sometimes we also have oatmeal porridge, which I hate!"

I shook my head in disgust thinking about it.

"We only have soup for lunch," I explained. "Do you think it's something you picked up from your relatives from El Táchira?"

Eva stopped walking.

"Do you have a problem with that?"

"Not at all," I apologized. "I was just curious. That's all."

"Are you sure you don't want to talk about Nazaret and Miss Carlotta?" Eva returned to the subject.

"Look, if I say something, she won't believe it, and then I'll get the rest of the class on to me," I worried. "I don't want that."

"My dad repairs her dad's car and he invited us all over for dinner on Saturday," Eva dropped in, casually.

"Are you going to Nazaret's home? Are

you friends with her?"

"No, dad thinks her dad will be good publicity for his garage that's all, so he wants us to go and support him," Eva reassured me. "Mom doesn't want to go either. You are my only friend and nothing is gonna change that, ok?"

I nodded in appreciation.

"Which is why I still think we should do something about her bullying you. I have a problem with that!"

"You are so sweet!" I said, hugging her. "But leave it, ok?"

"OK. By the way, how's the church thing going? Is the situation with your granny getting any better?

"What can I tell you? I get five cents every Sunday, but I'm tired of having to account for every breath I take, so I make up sins to have something to tell the priest, who, by the way, doesn't know the Bible that well!"

"What? A priest who doesn't know the Bible?" Eva asked, incredulously.

"Yes, I've caught him saying Mathew 29," I laughed. "But, there is no Mathew 29, for Christ's sake! Also, he always asks me to say three Lord's Prayers. Not two or one, always three. It never changes, no matter what I say."

"Caridad I didn't even know that there was a Matthew in the Bible. How do you know that kind of stuff, anyway?"

"I read it."

The school bell rang.

"That's the bell, we have to go," Eva interrupted. "See you at the break."

Then Eva merged in with the crowd on her way to class and disappeared into school.

**

"Nazaret! Where is my lunch bag?"

I grabbed the bully's arm, to make sure I got her attention.

"I don't know what you're talking about!" she said, shaking me off.

"I'm fed up with you hiding my lunch! Where is it?"

"Are you deaf? I don't know. Leave me alone!"

"I'm deaf, huh?"

I ran directly to her desk and searched around and underneath it for my lunch, without any luck. Then, I spotted her bag. Before she could stop me, I opened it in front of everyone. Nazaret ran over to stop me, but it was too late. She grabbed her bag and we pulled it back and forth. Finally, I let go and its contents flew in all directions. We stood there in the middle of the mess.

With the strength of a magnet, my eyes were attracted to a little package that read "Derby" in blue letters. I picked it up off the floor. Nazaret wasn't resisting in any way.

She stood there with an empty stare, as I picked up the rest of the books from the floor. And to my dismay, books and cigarettes were not the only things Nazaret had in her bag.

I picked up a magazine depicting a fat naked woman whose breasts were covered with strands of blonde hair. Her private parts were covered with a fig leave, and a snake was making its way up from her legs, while she was waving a bitten apple to a man who was hanging from an apple tree.

"This is so beautiful!" I said.

I held up the magazine the same way Granny Piedad had held up the toilet paper she had pulled from under my shirt the other day.

"I guess all this is yours," I added, mockingly.

I was about to hand her the whole stack of stuff, but it was too late. Someone had called Miss Carlotta, who now made her way through the ring of classmates circling us.

"Give me all that," Miss Carlotta snapped. "I want to see it!"

I looked at Nazaret and then handed the whole thing over to Miss Carlotta.

"It is my duty to inform the principal," she said. "We will not tolerate this kind of thing at school. Is this really yours, Nazaret?"

Miss Carlotta looked down at Nazaret in disappointment.

Nazaret whispered something inaudibly.

"What was that?" Miss Carlotta pushed.

"It was in my bag, so I guess is mine," Nazaret confessed.

**

"Father, I have sinned."

"Confess my daughter."

"I think I know who put a pack of cigarettes and a pulp magazine in Nazaret's bag."

"What kind of magazine is that?"

"Mom told me that they are a kind of bizarre comic with explicit language and sex scenes," I explained. "As usual, on Monday, my lunch disappeared. I knew Nazaret had something to do with it, so I confronted her and since she didn't give me my lunch back, I went to her desk to find it myself. I saw her bag and I thought that maybe she had hidden it in there. In the struggle to get her bag, everything in it ended up falling out all over the place, so the magazine and the cigarettes were there for everyone to see. She got suspended and it looks like she will be expelled."

"Was it you? Isn't that the girl you say you hate?" the priest inquired.

"No Father, it wasn't me and I don't know if I still hate her no."

"If you know who might have done this, then you should either talk to the teacher or confront the person. After all Nazaret is innocent!"

"Nazaret isn't innocent, Father!"

"You just told me that someone put those things in her bag."

"The other day, she ordered one of her lapdogs to step on my heel to take off my shoe on our way to gymnastics class," I pointed out. "And you know what? She succeeded. The problem was that I had a huge hole in the heel of my sock and they got to see it. Do you know what they called me after that? Little Orphan Annie!"

I heard another muffled sound from the confessional.

"Father? Father, are you really laughing?"

"Why were you wearing socks with holes?" the priest wondered. "You never know when you're going to have to take off your shoes!"

"Father I never imagined that they might step my shoes right off my feet," I explained. "Besides, it was the only clean pair of socks I had left. That's why she deserved the thing with the magazine! She's got lots of enemies!"

"By not saying anything, you are guilty as an accomplice. Did you know that?"

"What if I get into trouble? If I say something, I'm sure Miss Carlotta will believe I had something to do with it. Something else: Nazaret didn't even deny it!"

"My advice is this: Think about the

consequences!" the priest recommended. "Is there something else you want to tell me?"

"Yes, Father, I took one of my sister's bras. I put it on and filled it with toilet paper."

There was silence.

"Have you ever read the passage of the enraged dragon against the woman?"

"Yes, Father, I think it is described in Apocalypse--"

"13!" finished the priest.

"Actually, I think it was Apocalypse 12, Father," I corrected.

"Oh yes, sure you're right," the priest agreed. "Three Lord's Prayers and remember to talk to your teacher!"

"Amen, Father."

**

"Hi, sweetie! You've been hiding yourself away lately, I must say!" said Eva, with a touch of irony. "I hardly see you during the breaks, and I've called you a couple of times, but you haven't called back."

"You know how it is," I shrugged. "Homework, gathering sins for the confessional and all the tasks at home, I don't really have time."

I avoided her gaze.

"Today is the day, the bitch gets expelled," Eva rejoiced.

"Today?"

"What planet are you on? That's what everyone's talking about!"

"It was you, wasn't it?"

"My lips are sealed!" she said.

Eva made a cross with her fingers and smiled mischievously.

"I told the priest and he insisted that I should tell about the whole thing, 'cos if I don't, keeping quiet will make me an accomplice," I told her.

"So, what are you going to do?"

"I don't know…"

"Let me ask you something," Eva began. "Why do you think Nazaret didn't deny having anything to do with the packet of cigarettes?"

I didn't say anything. I had no idea.

"OK! Let me help you out," Eva interjected. "She smokes!"

"What?"

"Yeah, Nazaret smokes and I always knew it," Eva laughed. "Remember when I told you that nothing is what it seems? I had my suspicions and then we got the invitation to her place."

"So now you're telling me that she smokes at home?"

"Actually, that's exactly what happened," Eva explained. "Apparently, her dad, who owns the building where they live, converted the two apartments on the upper floor into one huge apartment, so she's got one of the wings to herself. They don't even bother to see what she's doing, as long as she doesn't leave the apartment alone."

"But you dropped the horrid pulp magazine in her bag, didn't you? I don't want her to get expelled for something she didn't do. That's all!"

"Keep your mouth shut, you hear me? Otherwise you and me will fall out, I promise you!" said Eva, pointing her index finger at my nose.

I lost it! I caught her finger with my teeth like a piranha from the Orinoco River. She yelped with pain.

"What's going on here?" asked Miss Carlotta, who had been standing nearby.

"Nothing, we're playing!" said Eva, holding her finger tight.

Eva was about to leave when the speakers sounded.

"Wait in rows, we have an important announcement to make!"

**

"Are you ill? You look pale," said Granny Piedad, touching my forehead.

"I think I've got a fever."

"Stay in bed, I'll ask Gustavo or Magdalena to go to church with me!"

**

"Mom, do you think Magdalena would like to accompany Granny Piedad to church?"

"What's happened? Did you have an argument with your grandma?"

"No, no. It's just that I don't have any sins left," I said, trying to make it sound casual.

"Then I don't see any reason why you should stop going with her."

**

"Father, I have sinned."

"Confess my daughter."

"I didn't say anything to the teacher about who put the cigarettes in Nazaret's bag."

"Can you live with the consequences of your silence?"

"Yes," I whispered.

"So you became your other classmate's accomplice. Is that what you're saying?"

"No, Nazaret didn't get expelled, on account of the outstanding marks she's got."

"Say one Lord's Prayer and think hard on what you've done!"

"Just one Lord's Prayer?"

"You heard me. Go with God!"

**

"Granny do you know if the priest ever confesses his sins?"

"Of course he confesses his sins! What kind of question is that?" she snapped.

Granny Piedad turned her head back to the bowl of black beans she was sorting for tomorrow's meal. The water in the pot was about to boil. I could hear José Luis Rodríguez singing "El Guía" on the radio.

Muy conforme con su suerte
En silencio uuuuna cruz llevaba
y callaba...

I was about to leave the kitchen.

"He confesses before God!" said Granny Piedad.

"Who? The priest? Wait a minute! Does he ever confess his sins before another priest?" I asked in disbelief.

"No, he is a priest! Why should he? He speaks directly to God!"

"Why can't we do the same?" I asked.

I felt the slap on the face, before I saw it. She hit me near my ear so there was a ringing sound in my head for a long, long time.

"Don't blaspheme like Dolores!"

Esperaba ser su guía aaaa.

José Luis Rodríguez was singing.

**

My mother leaned on the nightstand in our room as my sister played with her dolls.

"Magdalena, we have to send Caridad out of town," she began. "You know, to spend some time staying with Granny Mildred. The problem we have is who will take Granny Piedad to Mass on Sundays? We think you would be just perfect to do that. What do you think? You'll get five cents to buy whatever you want."

What No One Knew Of The Dead Man

"Matilde, I'd like to show you the leak under the sink in the men's rooms," said Régulo.

"Just a second."

Matilde raised her eyebrows in resignation. *At this rate, I'll never finish the letters don Adrián asked me to write*, she thought, as she headed to the men's room.

When she opened the door, Régulo pulled her into his arms and locked the door.

"Are you crazy? Can you imagine what will happen if someone finds us?" she said, feigning disgust.

"Relax, woman." He gave her a kiss on the nose. "I just wanted to know if you would join me and Santiago—you know him, my friend the lawyer, for a beer. Annnd maybe some more action for the two of us..." he whispered in her ear, as he rested his hands on her buttocks.

"Well, let me think about it... Oh, I almost forgot! Don Adrián wants to talk to you," she said, sliding her hand over his crotch. Without waiting for him to react, she opened the door and disappeared, satisfied at having heated his thoughts.

**

"Matilde told me that you wanted to see me."

Don Adrián jumped up and busied himself, trying to hide the deck of poker cards in his desk drawer.

"That's absolutely right, Régulo. Come in and lock the door. I want to ask you a favor..." He cleared his throat and settled his glasses on his nose.

"What would that be?"

"Do you know the financial statements you gave me the other day?"

"What about them?"

"Well..." don Adrián scratched his head, "the report is incomplete, as the maintenance expenditures are missing. I forgot to give them to you. The fault is mine," he hastened to say, as his eyes rested on a stack of folders lying next to the phone.

"No problem. I'll correct them on Monday first thing in the morn—" Régulo was already on his way out of the office when don Adrián interrupted.

"That's the problem; we can't wait so long. The director wants to have a look at the report before the shareholders' meeting... I was wondering if you could work on them this afternoon.

"You'll get paid overtime plus a bonus for saving my skin..." he added with a nervous smile.

"What about Casimiro? Why can't he add what's missing?" asked Régulo.

"I'd rather have you do the update since it was you who did the report," don Adrián explained, gaining ground.

Régulo nodded resignedly. "Don't worry, don Adrián;

I'll continue working on the report." Silently, he added, "I have no wife or kids waiting for me at home."

"Thanks, Régulo. I owe you one..."

"Would that be all?" asked Régulo, heading toward the door.

"That would be all, but remember the folders and bring them back when you finish the update, ok?"

"Oh, yes...of course." Régulo walked back to the desk, grabbed the stack of folders with both hands, and left the office.

When out in the hallway, he took a deep breath and headed for Matilde's desk.

"Sorry, honey. No beer tonight."

"What happened?"

"Ask don Adrián," said Régulo, returning to his desk.

**

Régulo put everything aside and began working on the folders he had taken from don Adrián's office. At first glance, it did not seem like much; but after a closer look, he realized that there was almost three months of unrecorded information.

He rolled his sleeves up and concentrated on the figures. Gradually, everyone, except him, left for home. The only things that could be heard in the office were the echo of the ticking clock at the entrance, the sound Régulo made while scribbling his notes, and the distant noise coming from the street.

The figures on the books began to dance before Régulo's eyes, and the heaviness in his head told him that it was time to take a break.

Régulo went to the canteen. He started the coffee machine and then headed, through the dark corridor to the bathroom.

"I guess that's how it is with don Adrián. Next time I'll just kick his sorry ass," he muttered while washing his hands. He went back to the canteen, hoping that the coffee was ready.

**

"Mo-om, the draw is about to start! Are you coming or not?" Dalia called from the living room.

"I'm coming, I'm coming! I'm in the bathroom..."

"Hurry up! It's starting now!" Dalia replied as she pushed Bent and Fisher off the couch. *These cats leave hair everywhere*, she thought, as she shook the cushions.

> *Good evening, Venezuela. A random selection of numbers may change your life forever. My name is José Arroyo Pedraza, and I'm here in RCTV's studio with Mr. Eusebio Montes to draw the numbers for the National Lottery.*
>
> *It's 7:58 today, Friday, 16th of April, 1976, and Mr. Eusebio Montes will be here with us in the capacity of notary public to confirm the transparency of the draw.*
>
> *Good luck, everyone! We are about to start. But before going any further, we must inform you that there were no winners last week.*

"Have they started?" asked Salomé. She was sitting in front of the TV screen, putting on her glasses.

"Almost. Tell Régulo he has to take his cats someplace else. Everything is covered in cat hair," Dalia complained.

"For Christ's sake, Dalia! These cats don't bother anyone! We all lose hair. Aren't they cute?"

"Shhh, they're drawing the lottery."

The third number from the National Lottery is sixteen. I repeat, sixteen. So, now we need to draw the very last number to get a winner.
Good luck, Venezuela. We are about to draw the last number here at The National Lottery at RCTV, today, Friday 16th of April, 1976.

"How are you doing?" inquired Salomé, trying to keep an eye on Dalia's ticket.

"Not even a single number," she replied, losing interest in the draw. "I'll finish watching it because of José Arroyo; I think he's hot," she added with a mischievous smile.

The fourth and last number for tonight's draw is four. I'll proceed to read the whole combination: seven, six, sixteen, and four. I'll hand the numbers to Mr. Montes for confirmation.
"Do you confirm?"
"I do."
Congratulations to the new winner. The winnings will be presented next week.
Good evening, and thanks for being here with us.

"I wonder if there's a winner... I better finish washing the dishes and go to bed," said

Salomé with a sigh while she took Fisher in her arms. The cat protested by purring.

At the bank office Régulo stared blankly at the wall after hearing the results of the lottery repeated on the radio.

"Seven, six, sixteen, four. Hell! That's my ticket..."

**

"Régulo, is that you? What happened to your keys?" she asked, afraid that the person on the other side of the door was someone else.

"Y'Can' find 'em."

Dalia looked out the window and saw Régulo. His face was red and his shirt off. Obviously, he was having a hard time keeping his balance.

"Dlia, Dlia op'n thdoor," he said, now leaning on the wall to keep from falling.

"Easy, Régulo! You're gonna wake the neighbors," said Dalia, hurriedly pushing the key into the keyhole to let him in.

When she opened the door, Régulo hunched over and, with awkward steps, he tried to hug her.

"Sis! Y'go' money. Y'go' money," he said, leaning his head on her shoulder while making circular movements with his index finger.

"You are drunk."

"So wha'? 'M fine now."

"Let me take you to your room before Mom sees you like this," she said, slinging his arm over her shoulder.

"What's happening here?" said Salomé.

"Nothing. It's just that Régulo is a little bit ill," answered Dalia.

"M-m-mom. Y'go' money. Y'go'... Y'go'money." He smiled with half-opened eyes, drool hanging from the corner of his mouth, and then his body shook. This was followed by violent retching as he let go of a stream of vomit that shot out like a water cannon. The damp odor of gastric acid and alcohol filled the room.

"'M sorry. 'M fine now."

"Take him to his bedroom. I'll clean this up," said Salomé with a grimace of disgust.

"Y'go'money," Régulo kept saying while Dalia dragged him all the way to his bedroom.

"Very nice of you!" Dalia roared the next morning, opening Régulo's door and turning on the lights. Régulo, who was lying awake in bed, broke wind that sounded like fireworks.

"This is what I think," he said, burying his face in his pillow.

Dalia got closer and snatched the blanket. The smell of burnt gunpowder rose from the bed, which made her move away quickly, covering her nose to repel the stench.

"What did I do now?" he asked innocently.

"What did you do? You got here drunk and puked in the middle of the living room! Are you going to sleep all day too?"

"Me?"

"Yes, you! And it was Mom who stayed up cleaning up your mess!"

"Do you know if there's milk in the fridge? This acidity is killing me," he said, holding his stomach.

"Yes! There is cold milk in the fridge, but you go and fetch it!" she retorted, crossing her arms.

Régulo turned to the nightstand, opened the drawer, and took out a piece of paper.

"I won!" he said, fanning the ticket near her face.

"What?" she asked, trying to snatch the slip of paper from him.

"Yes, I won the lottery," said Régulo, moving his hand away to avoid his sister's paw.

"Let me see it," she begged, but Régulo moved the ticket out of her reach.

"Serious?" inquired Salomé, who was standing by the door.

Régulo and Dalia stopped short and turned around to face their mother.

"Yes, Mom. I'm pretty sure, because when I bought the ticket, I laughed at the coincidence that the numbers were yesterday's date. Seven, six, sixteen, and four," he explained, as Salomé approached them with faltering steps.

"The year 76; one and six for the sixteenth; and four, the month of April," he continued. "And that's what I heard on the radio."

"You're talking about the National Lottery?" asked Salomé, with the severity of an undertaker.

"By any chance, do you have any aspirin?"

"We are talking about a thirty million dollar prize, right?" asked Salomé, ignoring Régulo's headache.

"Yes, Mom. Do you have any aspirin?" he replied, hammering the doorframe with a sudden movement.

"Let me see if I've got some left."

Salomé disappeared to get the pills, and then she called out from her bedroom. "I only have baby aspirin. You want some?"

"Yeah, just bring a couple of those."

"So that explains why you came home all wasted last night," Dalia said, poking him. "Let me see it."

"If you lose it..." he warned her.

"Do you think I'm so stupid?" She said this with a look of disappointment at his mistrust.

"You're right," he replied apologetically, and then he reached out and handed it to her.

From far away, the ticket looked more like a monopoly bill; but after a closer look,

Dalia recognized the good old 'NL' ticket. One could see that the image of the national hero in bright colors at the far end of the ticket filled a quarter of its overall size. At the bottom, it read, "Simón Bolívar (1783-1830) – Arturo Michelena" in very small caps.

Beside the picture, the following numbers appeared in large caps: Seven, Six, Sixteen, and Four. Right below was their equivalent in numerals, followed by the words "National Lottery" in bold red letters and then a short statement describing the date of the draw. At the bottom, there was a doodle, which obviously represented the signature of someone at the NL.

"Here," they heard Salomé saying behind them. She was holding a couple of pink pills.

"Look!" Dalia turned around to face her mom. "It seems all right," she said, handing her the ticket.

Salomé looked at it and then gave it a quick flip. She took a deep breath.

"I hope we keep this quiet," she announced sternly. "A least, until we get confirmation from the lottery office."

"I'll ask Santiago for legal advice on Monday."

"Don't say anything about your brother winning the lottery; otherwise, everyone will come here asking for money. So I'll say it again, we keep this quiet," said Salomé, looking first at Dalia and then at Régulo.

**

The alarm buzzed three times before Régulo deactivated it. It was 6:24A.M.

Peach shades announcing the new day bathed the room. He squeezed his eyes and stared at the wall. There was a *LIFE* magazine cover showing the image of a young man sitting in front of a chessboard. "The Deadly Gamesman," it said in bold print.

He smiled at the sight of the wet, sticky spot on his underpants and thought of Zenaida.

It had been five years ago that he'd gotten the flight ticket from don Adrián. His boss was supposed to have taken the trip to Rio de Janeiro, but he'd had another appointment in Liege that he could not decline at such short notice. So he'd decided to transfer the flight ticket to Régulo.

"What a woman," muttered Régulo. "What I wouldn't do to see her again! Yeah, I'm seeing Matilde, but it's not the same. Zenaida rocked my world. I'm glad I met her."

He closed his eyes for a moment and saw her as clearly as he had that day, waiting in line to embark on the cable car for a tour to Sugar Loaf. It was almost 6 o'clock in the evening.

The leaden sky had promised rain, but it had not happened. Her velvet dress with green and yellow stripes had matched her copper curls. On her neck, she'd worn the skin of something that appeared to be a foxtail, which had neither matched the weather nor the location.

Régulo had also noticed the red polish on her very short nails. There had not been much lipstick left, and the line she had drawn around her eyes had begun to run.

Zenaida had spoken perfect Spanish, except for the "você" that slipped from time to time, revealing her Portuguese roots. She had emphasized every word by brushing the fake fur around her neck, or stroking the cat she held, called "Shugarlouf."

The cat had reminded him of Bent, but Bent's fur was more golden, and he would not have allowed himself to be carried around in a bag.

Zenaida had looked at Régulo only once, and it had been enough. He'd invited her to have dinner, and she'd accepted on the condition that she would choose the place. By then, Régulo would have said yes to anything she'd proposed.

They had shared balls of black-eyed peas fried and stuffed with spicy pastes made from shrimp and ground cashews, which the locals call *acarajé*, in a restaurant on Rua Ministro Alfredo Valadão.

They had then crowned the night by wallowing like lizards in a pitch-black hotel room she'd chosen. Régulo had wished to try all sorts of juggling acts in bed with Zenaida, but she had insisted on being his Geisha. "Let me do the touching. Enjoy..." she had whispered.

They'd gotten drunk and wallowed on until the first light of dawn strained through the curtains.

Régulo had slept like a baby and had not noticed when she'd left, taking nothing else but his heart.

When he had come back to Venezuela, Régulo had contacted his old friend, the lawyer Santiago Pujol, so he could help Régulo with his last will. He wished to leave Zenaida his cats, his chessboard, his Suzuki van 125 bike, and anything else he had at the time of his death.

Santiago had tried to persuade him against this. In his eyes, it was absurd to leave everything to a person you had met only once.

"Boy! Are you nuts?" Santiago had asked in disbelief. "You got physical with a *garota*, and now you're gonna give her the cats?

You don't even have a place to drop dead." He'd then suddenly turned back toward Régulo and asked him, "Do you think I'm gonna do this for free because we're friends? What about your sister and your own mom? Don't they count?"

Régulo had burst out laughing, ignoring the comments about his sister and mother. "Not at all. I'm gonna pay you even if the will is more expensive than what she's gonna get." He gave him her address and smiled idiotically. "Her name is Zenaida Queiroz Gimaraes, and she smells like almonds."

Régulo snapped back to the present when the alarm clock buzzed again. It was 6:38A.M.; time to shower and go to work.

**

While heading to get the motorbike, Régulo strapped his helmet on. He found the bike where he had left it, with a blue plastic cover parked in the back alley. Régulo did not even wave back at his mother when he heard her blessing him from the window just before he left.

The city had not yet woken up. The bike roared good morning to his sleeping neighbors, spat a few puffs of smoke, and jolted forward. Régulo took a parallel route to the cemetery to get to the junction at La Bicentenaria Avenue, and then he rode over the old bridge to El Tambor Road.

The fog was thick and he could see no more than three meters ahead, so Régulo slowed down to 10km per hour and kept as close as he could to the right. Just millimeters separated him from the ditch.

Coming from the opposite direction, two headlamps appeared in his lane. Régulo tried to jump into the ditch, but the truck with red lettering "LN" was everywhere.

Everything happened so fast, Régulo thought for a second that it was a dream; the impact of the truck against the motorbike, feeling his own body being ejected into the windshield, the truck rumbling away as he lay in the gravel and glass. Blood, too much blood, streamed out of his mouth like a river. There were coughs, and then came the cold.

**

"Has anyone seen Régulo?" asked don Adrián from his office.

"No," replied Matilde from her desk.

"OK. When he comes, tell him to come into my office," he said, wondering what could have happened to Régulo why he hadn't left the folders on his desk as agreed.

**

Dalia turned on the radio to listen to the news while making breakfast for José Luis and Nino, who were almost ready to go to school.

We interrupt to report on the traffic. The exit of La Neblina, in the direction of the capital city, is closed both ways due to a car crash. There is one person dead. Apparently, the deceased was involved in a hit-and-run accident.

My God, that road is becoming more lethal than the Black Death, thought Dalia, cleaning up the kitchen after breakfast.

**

Knock, knock, knock on the door.

"Régulo, come in!"

"Don Adrián, it's me — Matilde," she said while opening the door with a worried expression. "There are two police officers who want to talk to you."

"Me? What do they want?"

"I don't know... They asked if Régulo Montoya works here. When I said 'yes,' they asked to have a word with you. Shall I bring them in?"

"Of course!" he said, standing and settling his tie.

**

"Just a second," said Salomé on her way to the door.

"Good afternoon. May we come in?" the taller of the two police officers asked.

Salomé looked them up and down to

confirm that they were actually law enforcement. The tall one was tanned with chalk-white teeth and had a glossy skull that was as polished as wet stone. The other, the smaller of the two, was like a tin soldier with rodent-like brown eyes and a pointy goatee.

What are they doing here? she wondered. The last time they'd come had been when Régulo had gotten drunk in a bar. It seemed that he'd attempted to use the sink as a toilet and had pulled the whole thing off the wall.

What has he done this time? she wondered.

"Come in, please," she said, stepping aside.

Salomé followed them into the living room and watched them expectantly.

"What happened?"

"Do you know Régulo Montoya?" inquired the shorter agent, as he read aloud from what appeared to be the ID card.

"I'm his mother." Her heart was galloping.

The police officer cleared his throat, dropped his head, and immediately said, "I'm sorry to say that he died in a road accident. The only identification he had was this card."

"What?" Salomé whispered.

"We need you to come with us to identify the body. We can escort you in case there isn't someone else who can take you there," the shorter agent added.

"I don't understand. Régulo went to work this morning... I heard him pull the motorbike out of the alley. I gave him my blessing. Did he ever make it to the office?"

The two officers merely shook their heads, as if on cue.

"It was a hit-and-run. The fog was thick this morning."

Salomé gave them a blank stare. Suddenly, she began to take short inhalations, as if she couldn't breathe.

"You don't understand... A mother shouldn't be allowed to identify the dead body of her son..." she said, shaking her head. She then sighed and fell onto the couch, covering her face with her hands.

**

"Matilde? Matilde?"

"What can I do for you, don Adrián?"

"Would you please walk the agents to the exit? And gather the rest of the staff in the canteen. I have an announcement to make.

"Thank you for coming," said don Adrián as he turned to the men at his side and shook their hands.

**

"Hello?"

"This is Mr. Pujol Cedillo's office. How can I help you?" the receptionist asked.

"May I speak to Santiago? Would you

please tell him that this is Dalia Montoya, Régulo's sister?" she said, wiping her nose.

"Just a second, please."

Dalia heard footsteps departing the reception area, and soon thereafter, she could hear them coming back.

"I'll put you through..."

Everything went mute and then a man's voice came through.

"Hello, Dalia... Is something wrong?" Santiago asked, feeling butterflies in his stomach, as every time he talked to her.

"Santiago, I'm very sorry to bother you..." Dalia paused and then sobbed, "I need you to accompany me to the morgue to identify Régulo's body."

**

"Hi, everyone. Thanks for coming at such short notice." Don Adrián took a deep breath and could not help noticing the blinking bulb of one of the lamps in the background.

"Today we've been informed that Régulo Montoya died in a hit-and-run accident."

Murmurs grew in the canteen, and both Casimiro and Matilde looked at each other in shock.

"I'll contact his family to find out about the funeral, so I'll keep you informed," added don Adrián with a severe expression.

He was about to leave the room when Casimiro asked, "May I take over his desk...now that he no longer needs it?" Casimiro looked puzzled, as he tried to understand why his teammates were looking at him disapprovingly. "I mean, he's got no use for it now, does he??"

"You're gonna need crutches if you don't shut up," Matilde hissed.

"Well, that was all I had to say," don Adrián added, ignoring Casimiro's remark.

"Matilde, please make sure the bereaved get a floral arrangement on our behalf. It should be sent to the funeral home."

**

Dalia took the local newspaper to check the obituaries section.

It was there as they had promised.

Régulo Montoya.
Age 39 - La Neblina
Régulo Montoya of La Neblina passed away on Monday, 19th of April, 1976. He was born in La Neblina to the late Eusebio P. Montoya.
Surviving are his mother Salomé Montoya, his sister Dalia Montoya, and his nephews Nino and José Luis Montoya.
Visitation will be held at the Bicentenaria

Funeral Home at 91 Junín St. on Tuesday, 20th of April, 1976. A service will be held at the funeral home on Thursday, 21st of April, 1976 at 10:30A.M. Interment will follow at the Municipal Cemetery, La Neblina.

Dalia checked to ensure that all the information was correct, and then she folded the newspaper and tucked it into her bag to show it to her mom, who'd spent the night at the funeral home.

Salomé kept her promise to not see her dead son, so she was seated on a chair by the entrance a few meters away from the open coffin, which was lying on a golden base in the middle of the chapel. On each side stood tall candles decorated with floral arrangements of white carnations.

She hated the lavish funeral Dalia had arranged for Régulo, because of its lack of modesty. In her eyes, this would send the wrong signal.

She loved her son, even though at times it was hard to like him. She could not help trembling at the thought of the last conversation she'd had with Dalia regarding the funeral.

"Mom, you don't understand! What will the neighbors say? That we are freaking cheap! Is that how we repay Régulo after he left the lottery fortune to you? We have ignored every single letter from people asking for money after news of his win. Are we really gonna bury him like a Mr. Nobody?"

"This burial is more expensive than the value of our own home," Salomé had said, pacing like a caged lion.

"It's true that we don't have the money now, but we will when the lottery formalities are fulfilled," Dalia had said, patting her mom's shoulder to reassure her.

Dear Lord, let the inheritance money come through as quickly as possible, Salomé thought as she stared at the coffin, and in that very moment Dalia came in.

Dalia spotted her mom from the entrance and went directly to her. She ran her hand through Salomé's hair, not only to caress her but also to tame her unruly locks.

"Did you see him?"

"Nope. I want to remember him like the last time we talked," Salomé said, fighting back the tears.

"The first guests are arriving. Why don't you go to the toilet and splash some water on your face? You look tired, Mom. Did you eat breakfast?" asked Dalia solicitously.

"Yes, I had toast and a cup of coffee."

"Good." She nodded and continued, "I wonder if you got many visitors yesterday."

"Yes, I'm very thankful." Salomé's eyes brightened. "Mr. Restrepo came early. You know him…the mechanic Régulo bought the motorbike from… And Mrs. Colina came along with her daughter." Salomé paused to remember who else had offered their condolences. "Oh, yes! Tito, who owns the shop near the cemetery. And Mr. Benito Luján…he also came, but that was very early today."

"I'm very glad you didn't have to stay all alone, Mom. I would have loved to stay here with you, but then who would have taken care of things at home?" she explained.

"Don't mention it. It's OK," she replied, patting her daughter's hand.

"Mom, don't you want to compose yourself a little bit? Remember that the service is at 10:30, and then we go to the cemetery."

"Yes, my dear, you're right. I'd better get ready." She stood up and left for the restroom.

Dalia approached the coffin to see her brother. He looked like a wax figure. Traces of cotton wad peeped out of his nose and his hands were resting on his chest, his intertwined fingers swollen and yellowish.

It was surreal… Last Sunday, she'd been bitching about him being drunk, and today this…

The sound of footsteps from the entrance took her out of her thoughts. She turned and recognized Casimiro, who had come with a woman and an older man. *They must be from the bank too*, Dalia thought.

"You must be Dalia. I'm Adrián Brito, Régulo's boss. I'm truly sorry for your loss," he said, shaking her hand.

"Thank you for coming." She nodded and then greeted Matilde.

"I gathered you were from the bank since I recognized Casimiro. You came home with Régulo once, remember?" she said, addressing Casimiro.

"Yeah, that's right, but it was a long time ago. Oh, by the way, I'm so sorry about Régulo..."

They stepped forward to look at Régulo. Matilde bit her knuckles to suppress the tears.

"Jeez! In spite of the blow, he looks the same!" Casimiro exclaimed.

"And not even your mom will recognize you if you open your mouth again, you hear me?" muttered don Adrián.

"Ejem...I'd like to greet your mom. Where is she?" he asked Dalia with a sigh.

"Sure, I'll show you..."

**

"Dalia, thanks for coming given the short notice," Santiago said, closing the door behind him. "Can I get you something before we start? Coffee, or perhaps water?"

"I'm fine, thank you, Santiago. Why couldn't we talk at home?" Dalia asked.

"Yes, we could have, but I didn't want to

distress Salomé...at least until we are completely sure..."

"Of what?" Somehow she sensed she would not like the answer. "There's something wrong with the inheritance, isn't there? Those bastards from the lottery won't pay because of Régulo's death, is that it?"

"Easy, Dalia. The first part of the money has already been transferred to his account."

"So what's the problem?"

"Yes, what's the problem..." Santiago drummed the desk with his fingers. "Well, the thing is that five years ago, when Régulo returned from Brazil, he asked me to register a will leaving everything he had to a lady he met in on his trip. Her name is Zenaida Queiroz Gimaraes."

"Are you serious?" she asked, jumping from the chair.

"Take it easy, Dalia," he said, gesturing for her to sit down.

"Yes, and I did as he asked me. At that time, it seemed unlikely that Régulo..." Santiago dropped his arms in hopelessness.

"Well, you know what I mean... The truth is that I did as he told me, which means that Zenaida gets everything." He rushed to add, "There is a small detail; Zenaida has to accept the inheritance, as stipulated by the civil rules. We have 180 days to establish the heir, so we have time."

"I've never heard of that woman. In fact,

I was convinced that Régulo wasn't interested in sex at all..." she sobbed.

"What makes you say that?"

"I mean, I'm his sister, and we used to talk a lot. I've never seen Régulo show interest in anything other than his motorbike, the lottery, and chess. Do you have any idea how many books on chess he had?"

"I guess he was very discreet."

"You have no idea how much my mom and I have put up with Régulo, or what we've spent on this funeral. If we don't pay, we will have to sell the house, and you know what? Even that won't be enough! Now you are telling me that he left everything to a woman he met just once? God damn you, Régulo!" She was in tears.

"I know it's hard, but there's still hope, because Régulo made the will but he never heard from her again. We might never find her, but we need to try. I will fly to Rio."

"I don't want to spend an extra nickel on Régulo. We're already up to our necks."

"Dalia, please calm down. The cost will be charged to the estate and unfortunately, we can't ignore the will. If you agree, I'll make a draft document where she gives up the fortune and makes Salomé the sole heir. What do you think?"

"I don't know of anyone who has given up a legacy of thirty million, but I guess we have no other choice but try to appeal to her conscience," said Dalia, lowering the corners of her mouth like a duck.

She was about to say something, but it was as if all the energy was suddenly drained from her. Instead, she picked up her bag and headed for the door.

"Go to Rio and do what you can," she said without looking back.

**

After nearly eleven hours of flying and a very short stopover at Tocumen Airport in Panama, Santiago arrived in Rio de Janeiro.

Thanks to his secretary, Santiago had reserved a room at the same hotel Régulo had mentioned in connection with the will five years before. This was the direction Santiago gave the driver when he was finally able to leave the airport.

At the hotel, Santiago could not help noticing the façade, despite the late hour. From what he could see, it was a two-story building of roasted-yellow walls. The windows and the verandas were white. The wall of the ground floor was covered with arabesque tiles that may well have been blue or black. Daylight would reveal the answer.

He paid the driver and knocked on the front door. A short, plump, suntanned man opened it. He seemed to be in charge. Santiago explained that he had a reservation, and after taking a look at the books, the man confirmed that everything was all right.

The man insisted on carrying the only bag Santiago had brought with him. They climbed a narrow staircase with black railings and wooden steps, and then they turned left. Down the hall was room number seven. The man opened the door, and then he gave the keys to Santiago. He stayed for a few seconds as if waiting for something. Santiago realized that he must have been awaiting a tip, so he gave him ten cruzeiros. The man flashed a huge smile and disappeared down the hall.

Santiago was tired and queasy, so he decided to wait until the next day to start making his inquiries. He lay on the bed and fell asleep.

When he awoke the next morning, he realized that he hadn't taken his clothes off. It was 9:47A.M. He took a shower.

Santiago couldn't help but he concerned by Dalia and Salomé's financial situation. Régulo had been very persuasive, and even though it was crazy, he had helped him to leave Zenaida and Salomé in a bad situation. A part of him wanted to tear up the will and forget about it; but he was a lawyer, and his name was everything to him. He had to do the right thing.

Once he was ready, Santiago went to the reception area of the hotel. His stomach rumbled, reminding him that he had not eaten since he'd gotten off the plane.

"That can wait," he muttered, as he approached the counter. A woman who looked to be close to her forties smiled as he approached her.

Her Spanish was a bit more understandable than that of the man he'd spoken to the night before, so without further ado he asked her about Zenaida.

When she heard the name her smile turned into an expression of disgust. He explained to her that he was a lawyer and that he really needed to talk to Zenaida, or any of her family members, regarding an important legal matter.

She looked at him suspiciously and picked up the phone, buzzing the manager who had helped him the night before.

When he came they engaged in a discussion of which Santiago did not understand a single word. Finally, the man led him away from the receptionist, who looked watched their departure with a glower.

Santiago asked if he knew Zenaida. The man explained that he knew her well but that she had been kicked out when the previous owner had learned that she was ill.

Zenaida was an escort, and the hotel was where she brought her clients. Until she grew too sick to work they'd never had problems with her; apparently she paid good commission and everyone was happy with the agreement. The man was almost sure there was still a bag with some of her belongings in the garden shed.

The man was more than willing to show Santiago the bag, likely hoping to get a handsome tip for the favor, so he took him along the corridor and through the kitchen, which buzzed with activity. The strong smell of cocoa embraced them until they exited through a door leading to the backyard, which was filled with trashcans and cleaning paraphernalia. Toward the left corner there was an open metal door. They went in.

The place was slightly dark and was packed with junk; all kinds of objects hung from the roof and cluttered the floor. They made their way through the cramped space towards a corner that contained a pile of plastic bags. The man began to open them, the first, a second, and then a third. To Santiago's dismay, he found nothing. He looked around and seemed to spot a couple of bags under a chair. He pulled them out and rushed to open the first one, but by the disappointment on his face, Santiago could see it was the same outcome. The man then took out the one at the bottom of the pile.

"*Isso...era o que restava de Zenaida,*" he said, his face brightening with a smile. He seemed totally unaware that Santiago didn't speak Portuguese.

He handed Santiago the bag, and this time, Santiago gave him 100 cruzeiros. From what Santiago understood, he could keep the stuff. They walked the whole way back in silence, parting ways in the lobby.

Santiago took the flight of stairs two by two, praying that he had not wasted his money. Pouring the contents of the bag onto the bed, he began to rifle through the jumble of clothes, shoes and cheap jewelry.

There was also a fuchsia boa, something like a foxtail and a brown clutch. An almond fragrance permeated the
room and made him recall his conversation with Régulo.

Santiago pushed the clothes and shoes aside and then did the same to the underwear, the boa, and the foxtail. He checked the bag once more to make sure that nothing had been missed.

"I just paid 100 cruzeiros for a bunch of crap," he muttered.

Santiago sat on the bed to catch his breath and felt a lump against his back. It was the clutch.

Jumping up he took the small bag and opened it. It had two compartments of equal size and a little zippered pocket. Inside was a round bottle with a gold cap like the end of a trumpet. It had a black tag that read "French Almond Eau de Toilette."

He opened the pocket and found a little

book filled with names and phone numbers. When he flicked through it a business card fell to the floor. Apart from that, there was nothing else, no money, no ID. He picked up the card.

>   Rodrigues e Carvalho - Advogados
>   Ive Gomes Filho
>   Rua Joachim de Sousa, 1572
>   Rio de Janeiro–RJ
>   21540-370
>   Tel. (21) 2205 6270

He looked at the back, but there was nothing written there. Walking around the room, he wondered what the hell he was going to do. He had a book with hundreds of phone numbers and a card. Santiago did not know whether to laugh or cry. If he were to check every single phone number, it would take him days to finish. What if they were only one off clients and nothing else?
The card is the winner, he thought.
There was no phone in the room, so Santiago went down to the reception area, hoping to make the call in private. He approached the counter and saw that there was a couple checking in. He waited what seemed like an eternity.
When his turn came he explained to the receptionist that he needed to call the number on the card. She pointed to the back of the

room.

"Only local phone calls are free of charge."

"It's a local call," he said, waving the card.

The gray phone was on a round table in a corner of the room. Santiago took up the receiver, waited for the tone, and then dialed the number, *Beep, beep, beep, beep* without pause.

He tried again without including the international code. There was a series of long beeps, and on the third beep, a woman said something that sounded like, "*Gódrigues y Carfállo, Ayívogados.*"

"*Habla español?*"

"Yes, of course. How can we help you?" Her Spanish was perfect.

"May I speak to Mr. Ive Gomes Filho? I believe he's a lawyer."

"He's not in at the moment. May I take a message?"

"Sure. My name is Santiago Pujol Cedillo. I'm a lawyer from Venezuela. I'd like to discuss a private matter with him."

"Do you have a phone number he can call?"

"Just a second." Santiago ran over to the counter to get a card with the hotel's number. He felt awkward about being unprepared for the call. "Sorry to make you wait."

"No problem at all," she said.

He gave her the number and stressed that it was urgent.

After the phone call ended Santiago had a mixture of feelings. Somehow he knew that everything depended on that call, if it didn't lead to anything he'd be lost.

The hours passed and at midday he decided to go to the hotel restaurant to get something to eat. He left a message at the reception desk so they would know where to find him.

Santiago was gulping a second serving of a dish of black beans, chopped sausages and rice when the receptionist waved at him from the restaurant entrance. He had a call.

"Hello?"

"Hello, this is Ive Gomes. I understand from my secretary that you called me..."

"That is correct. I'd like to talk to you in person. It's about a woman called Zenaida."

Ive Gomes stiffened and replied, "I don't know what you're talking about."

"I think you know pretty damned well what I'm talking about. If you don't want to see me, I will show up at your office.

How's that sound?" growled Santiago, half perplexed by his own reaction.

"Is not what you think." He paused, "Zenaida was my sister!"

"Oh," said Santiago apologetically. "Please allow me to explain. It is about an inheritance of which she is a beneficiary."

"Which hotel are you staying at?"

Santiago gave him the information and the lawyer promised to be there within the half hour.

He put the phone back and returned to the restaurant to finish his lunch, but the beans were cold and he was too jumpy to eat. He left the dish and went back to the lobby to wait for Mr. Filho.

Santiago heard footsteps coming from the entrance of the hotel and spotted a thin man with a light complexion and red hair.

He was dressed in a safari-like jacket, his collar open down to a hairless chest that boasted a gold chain and crucifix.

They made eye contact and the man walked the last few steps with confidence.

"You must be Santiago," he said, leaving Santiago with his hand outstretched.

"Please accept my apologies for the way I just spoke to you on the phone." Santiago dropped his hand. "I had no other way of contacting your sister... Do you think I can talk to her?"

"Don't worry about it," he said, waving his hand dismissively. "You won't be able to talk with her."

"Maybe you've heard about Régulo Montoya. I'm here on his behalf..."

The lawyer walked a few steps forward and Santiago followed.

"Zenaida passed away almost two years

ago."

"What? I'm sorry for your loss. May I ask you what happened?"

"The doctors don't know," he said. "Apparently it all started with a high fever and a stomach ache and then blotchy skin. She looked like a leopard the last time I saw her..." he said, grimacing at the painful memories. "They kept her tied to the bed to restrain her from attacking the nurses," said the lawyer, staring at the floor. "In the end, I stopped visiting."

There was an awkward silence.

"I need to know if you are going to claim the inheritance."

"I'm pretty sure we don't want that kind of money."

"It's a large sum of money..." Santiago insisted.

"I wouldn't care if it were one hundred million. I don't know how much you've learned about my family, but we are very wealthy. My parents are highly thought of in the Church, and they will never accept money from Zenaida. She has done nothing but tarnish the family name."

"Well then... I need to prove that she is dead, and that there won't be a claim from your family on this matter."

"Don't worry. I will instruct my secretary to send you a copy of the death certificate and a renunciation statement. I have power of attorney, which allows me to act on my family's behalf," he assured him.

"Where was she interred? I'd like to lay some flowers on my friend's behalf, if you don't mind."

"No problem at all. She was buried in São João Batista Cemetery here in Rio." He was about to leave, and then he changed his mind and turned back.

"There's something else you should know."

**

"Santiago, tell me you have good news. The people from the funeral parlor are about to go crazy. They want their money!" Dalia exclaimed, lying on the couch in Santiago's office.

"Very good news indeed! Salomé is the heir because Zenaida passed away almost two years ago, and her siblings gave up their rights to the inheritance. I have both the death certificate and the renunciation in my possession."

Dalia applauded upon hearing the good news and, without thinking about it, threw her arms around Santiago's neck and kissed him on the shoulder.

Santiago embraced her too. He closed his eyes for a second while taking a slow, deep breath.

"Was she easy to find?" Dalia asked, suddenly feeling awkward.

"I didn't even have to leave the hotel," said Santiago. "There was a bag with some of her stuff and I found a little book with a card from someone who happened to be her brother," he said, leaning on the edge of his desk.

"Ohhh, what a relief!" Dalia smiled, clapping her hands with joy. "I'll pay you handsomely."

"Something else..." He paused trying to find the right words. "Zenaida's real name was Renato...Renato Gomes Filho."

"Renato? Isn't that a male name?"

"Yes. Zenaida, or Renato, was born as a male and comes from a wealthy family. Renato was an escort. Her family gave up their rights to the fortune in order to avoid scandal. I think it would be best if you don't mention any of this to your mom. Don't you think?"

**

After the conversation with Santiago, Dalia felt her muscles relax in relief. She was young and free. Everything was resolved; they would pay the funeral debt, and there would be no need to count every single nickel they spent. *Everything has a price*, she thought.

"This money came to us as a blessing,"

Dalia muttered, as the tears streamed uncontrollably. She had lost her brother, his memory steeped in disloyalty and selfishness. There was no happiness; only a deep sorrow that Régulo left everything to a person he hardly knew. What about his mother and herself? Apparently, they amounted to nothing in Régulo's world.

They'd both been there every time he'd been drunk and had puked on the carpet, or wet the bed. To think that everything would have gone to Zenaida if she had not died first.

Dalia thought of going straight home but then she changed her mind when she was passing by Tito's shop.

She went in.

"Hello, Tito! Mom told me you were at the funeral parlor... I just wanted to say thanks."

"Don't mention it. How's Salomé?"

"You know how it is..."

"Give her my love. Don't you fancy some malt? My treat," he said, trying to cheer her up as he noticed her tears.

"Yes, thanks." She took his gift and nodded at the back wall. "How much is that bunch of pink carnations?"

"Are they for Régulo?"

She nodded, wiping her nose with her sleeve.

"I have some white, if you prefer..."

"Pink!" she snapped.

He took them from the bucket and wrapped them in newspaper.

"What do I owe you?"

"Maybe another time," he said, looking down.

"Sorry I barked at you... It's been hard lately..."

"I understand. Hurry up; they will close soon," he said, pointing toward the cemetery gates.

"Thanks, Tito!"

"Go with God," he murmured.

Dalia hurried in the direction of the gates. There were few visitors to the cemetery at this time. *Tito was right; they must be about to close*, she thought, heading in the direction of Régulo's grave.

She went straight ahead and took a left, where they buried the "rich," she'd been told. It had rained a few hours before and the earth was damp. Dalia continued about fifty steps to a side corridor and stopped in front of Régulo's grave.

They had already begun to lay the marble gravestone, but there was much to do yet. She stood there for a few seconds, looked around, and took three steps forward to stand where she supposed Régulo's head would be.

The earth felt soft, like cushions beneath her shoes. The wind was still. All she heard was a flock of pigeons flying in the distance.

Dalia did not care that her shoes were

getting muddy. She looked around to see that no one was looking. With disdain, she tossed the pink carnations on the grave.

Spreading her legs, she tucked her hand under her skirt and pulled her panties aside. A blast of cold air surged between her legs. She looked around once again to make sure no one was watching.

With that last confirmation she closed her eyes, relaxed her muscles, and emptied her bladder.

"Rest in peace," Dalia whispered, as she let it all out.

Presumed Indecent: The Story Of Maruja Colina

PROLOGUE

Mirella and Gaspare Pellegri lived in Taormina, a town on the east coast of Sicily. Inseparable since childhood, there was no surprise when they announced they were getting married. They bought the only hotel in town, which they renamed Corso Umberto. Flourishing with their hard work, it eventually became one of the most prestigious lodgings in the area. Although in many ways, Mirella and Gaspare had it all, they didn't have children. They were both in their forties when they began to lose faith.

At the end of each day, Mirella would sit beside the window complaining to God that she had become a "barren hen." Gaspare tried to comfort her until it was very clear that she was not going to be getting pregnant, and then they both gave up. Then, when they least expected it, Mirella discovered that God had delivered a miracle.

The baby girl was born at only eight months. She was fragile, but lovely. Her skin had a fine fuzz, not unlike the skin of a peach, and lively honey-colored eyes filled her face. They called her Franca.

Franca soon became the family treasure. Who would have ever thought that the little girl who ran around her parent's hotel playing maid with her friend Tomaso Lombardi would become a young woman with the beauty of a goddess?

Although Mirella and Gaspare were well aware of the emotions their daughter aroused in men, they were certain that Franca would one day marry Tomaso. Indeed, they weren't the only ones; everyone in town assumed that one day the two of them would end up exchanging rings at the cathedral.

Then, in the summer of 1974, Cesare Piccio came to Taormina. A beautiful young man, he was well dressed, with a feline gait. He came to stay at the hotel and soon became known in town for his generous tips.

Franca felt lightning strike her for the first time in her life and a tickle in her stomach kept her awake at night. Never before had she encountered a man of Cesare's stature. Before this, Franca had always thought that her life was settled, that she would marry Tomaso, and that they would continue on forever, together with the hotel. Now she was not so sure. She could not resist Cesare's honey curls and the feline way he walked. His green eyes could paralyze her instantaneously. Sometimes, she scolded herself for her weakness and began making detours to avoid him.

The lightning fell also upon Cesare; with the patience of a fisherman, he spied on her from the window of his room. Watching her closely when she wasn't looking, he smiled to himself with certainty that sooner or later she would be his. Not wanting to rush things, he invited her for a stroll along Corso Umberto in broad daylight. It worked, and before long, they were taking long rides all over Taormina on a rented scooter.

They rode as far as Isola Bella just to hear the waves licking the shore. Cesare kissed her hands, and they became increasingly intimate until it was too late to stop.

As far as Tomaso was concerned, Franca was the love of his life. Sometimes they strolled, holding hands, along the Corso Umberto passage. At other times, they discussed the idea that the passage would attract more tourists if there were some kind of religious monument. They used to joke that what the famous passage really needed, was the image of the Mother of Jesus, but that was long before Cesare came along.

Since Cesare took the town by storm, Tomaso and Franca barely spoke to each other and she was nowhere to be seen at the hotel. Tomaso could not help but acknowledge the charm of a well-travelled person such as Cesare. He loved her unselfishly, and hoped that Cesare would love her forever and crown her as a queen.

And crown her Cesare did, Franca blew the news unwittingly when she protectively covered her stomach. All of a sudden, Cesare did not have time for long rides on the Vespa, and there was no trace of him to be spotted downtown. Franca had grown up in a loving home. Surrounded by tender, caring people, she had no reason to believe that he was playing. Thus, she decided to wait until Cesare proposed. She toyed with the idea of staying at the hotel with him, to lend a hand until Mirella and Gaspare retired.

As for Cesare, Franca became a real nuisance, and why not say it? She was slightly too needy for his style. To make matters worse, as he had suspected, there was a "bun in the oven." She confirmed it that night over cannoli.

"We can make arrangements to get married as soon as possible. What do you think?"

His laughter was like a whip, as he mocked, "Are you sure that baby isn't Tomaso's?"

All of a sudden Cesare's patience and good manners were gone; the change was so profound and to such a degree, Franca felt as if she were talking to a Mafioso. For a second, she thought that he was joking, that he soon would take her into his arms and reassure her that everything would be fine, but he didn't.

That was the last time they saw each other. He dropped her off at the hotel and the next day he was gone. He didn't even pay his bill.

Franca decided to talk to Tomaso, who listened to the whole story with clenched fists. He proposed to her and offered to take care of the child and make it look as if he were the real father. Franca was touched by the gesture, but still believing that Cesare would eventually apologize and propose, she would never have accepted such a thing. Nonetheless, as the days came and went and the summer was dying, she realized that Cesare had merely notched up another trophy.

Tomaso secretly enquired about Cesare's whereabouts. That was how he learned that "Cesare Piccio" was most likely a fictitious name and that the jerk didn't even live in Italy. Cesare, or whatever his real name was, had embarked somewhere in Latin America.

Franca was consumed with shame and heartbreak. Mirella and Gaspare tried to convince her that the child was a blessing, but she became more and more disconnected from the world. She stopped eating, and as soon as night fell, she wandered the streets of Taormina in search of Cesare. Tomaso, Mirella, and Gaspare took turns getting her back.

Then, one cold mid-autumn night, no one could find her. After two days of intense searching, Tomaso begged the police to let him break the news to her parents. They had found Franca's body floating along the beach at Isola Bella.

Although Tomaso thought his life was over, now that he knew all about Franca's death, it gained a sense of direction. Before going to bed each night, he knelt before the image of a framed Virgin Mary hanging in his room.

"Give me Cesare Piocci and I'll honor your image," he prayed quietly.

1976

Character is like a tree and reputation like a shadow.
The shadow is what we think of it;
the tree is the real thing.
Abraham Lincoln

Two girls dressed as angels tossed rose petals to the floor as they made their way to the altar. Behind them, Enzo led Maruja, his wife-to-be, down the aisle of the church. The wedding would have been perfect if it weren't for the ever-foggy weather of La Neblina. It was midsummer and thick layers of mist covered the landscape. It would have been perfect if Viktor-Walter had not been infatuated with Uncle Piero's wig.

While the bride and groom stood waiting for the priest, a tumult was heard among the guests. Viktor-Walter put his paws on the pew, jumped, and ran away with the trophy hanging from his muzzle.

It was memorable to see Piero running after the dog of one of the guests to retrieve his stolen hair. Many of the attendants covered their mouths with their hands to hide a smile or stifle a laugh. Uncle Piero took it gracefully though; he regained his wig, patted Viktor-

Walter on the head, and bowed, giving permission for the ceremony to continue.

Once Enzo and Maruja were declared husband and wife, they left the church through a shower of confetti and released doves – a symbol of their love and happiness.

The old Rolls Royce in which they drove to the wedding reception was decorated with balloons and ribbons of white silk. The party was held in Fiume Veneto, a club that belonged to the Italian community in La Neblina. Round tables were set on both sides of the room; the chairs were covered in white satin and pink ties; and the glassware reflected the golden flashes from the chandeliers. There were antipasti, Italian soups, and Italian sweets. Enzo's family toasted with a very Italian cry of *"evviva gli sposi."*

Amanda was ecstatic on Maruja's behalf. Every chance they got, they sat together to chat. "Dear, you can come back to us if you don't like it, ok?"

"I'll be fine, you'll always be like my real mother," Maruja reassured her, patting her hand.

Mateo joined them, holding a glass of champagne.

"Enjoy your party. Maruja, I'll take care of this beautiful lady. Tell me that I'm not lucky for having such a wonderful wife?" Mateo said, passing his arm under hers to lead her to the dance floor.

"I'm the lucky one for having you both in my life," Maruja answered. "You always took such great care of me, thank you both!"

"Go! Enjoy your party, I'll take care of her," Mateo responded in an attempt to conceal his own worries. Although he wasn't nearly as emotional about the celebration as his wife was, from his perspective, this was nothing more than a circus set up by Enzo and his family.

Maruja already knew that he was uneasy because they were not able to bring a single Spanish touch to the festivities.

"That's ominous," he would repeat at every opportunity. "If this is how it is now, just imagine when Maruja signs the marriage certificate."

Although she hadn't wanted to fuel the fire, Amanda had also watched with concern as Enzo and his family expanded their influence over every single aspect of the wedding. The initial agreement had been that Mateo and Amanda would take care of the church, and Enzo's family the reception. But soon the Italians were choosing the church, the reception, and even the wedding dress and honeymoon destination.

**

Enzo and Maruja went directly to their hotel room after the party. When Enzo turned on the lights, they were greeted by a pristine white decor. In the center of the room, a large bed was draped romantically in white and pale green cloth. Deep red rose petals, identical to those at the wedding, were scattered across the bed. Among them was a swan. Taking a greeting card out from under its wing, Maruja picked up the plush bird, "Have a happy life!" it wished them in a large, curly font.

"How do you like the room?" he asked.

"I love it, it's just perfect! Thank you, Enzo. You never skimp on expenses to make me feel like a queen," Maruja said. Although reassuring her husband, she was somewhat afraid that he might attack the bellboy, as he had in the restaurant just moments before. He had no tolerance for servants. Maruja had dropped a casual comment that the meal would have been perfect if they could have served it warmer. To her horror, Enzo had slapped the waiter when he dared to blame the chef.

However, when she saw Enzo's smile, Maruja spun around with open arms, before falling onto the bed. She closed her eyes. It seemed unbelievable that so many months of preparation had finally culminated in the most beautiful wedding party the city had ever witnessed.

Enzo walked around the room like a big cat – opening doors, testing water taps, and checking the windows. The stress of the past month had taken their toll on him too, but thank God everything was over and tomorrow they would be flying to Maui for the honeymoon.

"*Cara mia.*"

"Yes, my love?" Maruja answered from the bed, beckoning him to come lay with her.

He turned the lights back off and joined her. She stared at him, her heart beating furiously. Enzo's green eyes seemed to burn through her without a touch. She could not help but to admire the twisted honey strands of her husband's hair. It was only a few hours before, that this very man had become her husband. She still couldn't believe how lucky she was. Although they had been together for more than a year now, the feeling persisted of being just a little thing for a man such as him, as though she weren't good enough.

**

Covered by the gray tulle of darkness, they made love. When finished, Enzo turned his back on her. "You're not a virgin," he muttered.

"What? We've been making love for the last eight months. Why are you saying that?" She put her hand on his shoulder to make him turn around.

"You should have stopped me back then, made me wait until we were married... You should have shown more character, more strength... I'm just saying that you married me without being a virgin. Technically, you're a slut," he replied with a smile.

Maruja looked at him without knowing whether he was serious or not. After a moment, she dared to ask, "Don't you think it's a little late for such considerations? Why didn't you talk about this before?"

"Let's play. Perhaps I should punish you for being cheap," Enzo replied, ignoring her question. He jumped out of bed and picked up his pants. In one movement, he pulled the belt from the trouser loops and rolled it twice around his hand.

"Kneel!" he commanded.

"Enzo, I'm too tired to play games." Maruja replied, shaking her head. "Come lie down with me and stop talking like that." A bad feeling was growing in her stomach. Before she could react, the belt cut through the air and tore into her naked shoulder one, two, three times.

"Stop!" she cried with a mixture of horror and surprise.

"Kneel!" Without waiting for her response, Enzo pulled her hair and forced her onto her knees. She began to cry and he slapped her. Then he strode around the room, muttering under his breath in Italian as he swung the belt at her.

Maruja tried to run for the door, but Enzo

reached out and pulled her back.

"This can't be happening," she whispered between sobs.

"You whore! You've made me into a sinner!" He screamed, making a knot on the end of the belt, and walking toward the corner of the room. Maruja tightened her lips and shut her eyes, awaiting the next hit, but it never came. Slowly, she looked up and saw her husband still standing in the corner, his arms outstretched like a crucifix. The belt in his right hand lashed over his shoulders again and again.

Maruja tried to stop him, but Enzo pushed her aside and kept swinging until he fell down at her feet in exhaustion.

"Please forgive me, Maruja! I am a sinner," he whimpered, his face buried in her feet. "It will never happen again, I promise."

She stood him up and led him back to the bed, where he laid his head on her lap. Although Maruja stroked his hair, there was a chilling lack of emotion in the act. She felt surprise and emptiness; she felt lost. The man to whom she had just vowed to commit her life now seemed so alien; she may as well have been stroking a cabbage. Tears ran nonstop from both of their eyes.

Maruja was convinced that the best course of action would be to get out of Enzo's life. Yes, run away, and do it as soon as possible. Otherwise, the same old story she had watched unfold as a little girl would repeat itself with her.

Thanks to Mateo and Amanda, Maruja had been given the chance to become a normal person with a decent life. No way would she immerse herself in those horrors again. Back then, she couldn't do much, but now she was a grown-up. She wouldn't let any man do to her what they had done to her mother, who had ultimately ended up disappearing without a trace.

What just happened here? Maruja wondered as she watched her new husband sleeping. Just a few seconds ago, he had been swinging the belt around on him and her alike. *This isn't normal. Yes, Enzo sometimes has this horrid temper with others, but me?* He had always treated her like his very own Madonna.

Maruja waited a little longer, and then she moved his head away. She covered him with one of the lovely pastel green sheets, picked up her handbag and clothes and slipped out the door.

**

"My God! What happened?" One of the maids had been carrying a cooler to some of the guests, but when she saw the half-naked woman scrambling down the hall, she dropped it and ran to see if she could help. She led Maruja to a storeroom near the elevators. "You can get dressed here without people eyeing you," she said, before walking out, leaving the door ajar.

Maruja changed her clothes and headed for the lobby.

"What can I do for you?" the receptionist asked, thinly veiling her shock.

Even dressed, Maruja still looked rough. "I'd like you to call a taxi," she replied, either not noticing or caring about the distress in the worker's voice.

"Of course, ma'am, right away."

"Hurry up, please," she said, looking nervously back into the hall.

"Perhaps you'd feel more comfortable sitting here while you wait." The receptionist pointed to the office at the back of the desk.

Fearing that Enzo could come after her at any moment, Maruja agreed. The office was not as small as she had anticipated. There were two desks facing each other, and two phones. Folders were stacked in perfect order. A whiteboard was the only thing hanging on the wall. There was also a water cooler and a tower of plastic cups.

"Do you want something to drink?"

"Yes, please."

Almost as soon as she had a cup of water in her hand, the sound of an engine could be heard outside the hotel. The receptionist went out to check. "The taxi is here," she reported.

Maruja rushed to the exit. The worker

escorted her, looking toward the stairs to make sure no one came in their direction.

The driver opened the door and let the battered newlywed in. "Where are we going?"

"I don't know, just far from here."

**

"Maruja?" Enzo called from the bed.

The sun streamed through the curtains in the quiet hotel room. Enzo looked around and flashes of the events from the night before came to his mind. The party, the tarantellas he danced with Maruja, all the Amaretto he drank, the arrival at the hotel, and the punishment...

At first, he thought that Maruja was in the bathroom, but when he got no answer from her, he rested on his elbow and eyed the room. When he noticed that her handbag was missing, he jumped out of bed and decided to confirm what he already knew.

His deep breath echoed against the walls of the empty bathroom. With certainty that he was now alone, Enzo put on his clothes from the night before, splashed some water on his face, and left.

**

"What are you doing here? I thought you were heading to Hawaii."

"Maruja left me," Enzo said, pushing his younger brother aside. He continued straight to the kitchen, looking for Concetta. "Where is Mamma?"

"No idea. She said where she was going, but I didn't pay attention. She couldn't be far..." Gino said, scratching his head before returning to the previous topic. "Why would she leave you?"

Enzo ignored the question and kept searching throughout the house for his mother. He was about to leave when Albano and Concetta appeared and exchanged glances of astonishment.

"What in the name of God are you doing here? I thought you were in Maui!"

"Mamma!" he yelled, throwing his arms around her. "I punished her cos' she wasn't a virgin. I had planned to send her back to her parents this morning, but when I woke up, she was gone."

"What do you mean by 'punished her?'" Albano asked.

"She's not a virgin, so she deserved the couple of lashes I gave her."

"Lashes! Are you nuts?" Gino asked from the kitchen door.

"Gino, mind your own business!" Enzo snapped.

"Maruja might be your wife, but you have to talk to her family," his father admonished.

"Let him speak!" said Concetta.

"There's not much to say, Mamma. She isn't a virgin and I don't want her back. That's what you guys have to say to anyone who comes here asking questions. Are we clear?" Enzo looked around at all of them.

"Sure, bambino." Concetta spoke as though she were talking to a little boy. Then she looked at her husband to get his consent. "*Caro*, I told you that it wasn't a good idea to marry her, a girl with her descent..."

"What if Mateo and Amanda come here asking questions? They're like her parents," Albano asked, visibly worried.

"They won't come. I guess they would feel ashamed of having such a daughter."

"You mean you're not going to talk to them?" Albano was unable to hide his disapproval.

"If they come, I'll talk to them. Otherwise, I'll leave it at that."

"My point is that *you* should take the initiative, don't you see this?" Albano asked, pointing at his son.

"I don't care."

"YOU OWE THEM AN EXPLANATION!" Albano shook his arm free from Concetta's grip. "You didn't learn that crap from this family, do you hear me?" He added, slamming the dining table.

Albano took a deep breath and approached his son, who was watching him open-mouthed. "I'm not going to clean up your mess like I did with that poor girl you ruined two years ago. You insisted on marrying Maruja, now you go and YOU explain it to Mateo and Amanda. I don't care if they aren't her real parents!"

Enzo slammed the door on his way out.

**

"The Golden Stork. How can I help you?"
"Mom?"
"Maruja, is that you? Where are you? People are saying terrible things about you! Is it true that Enzo dumped you?" Amanda asked, looking around to make sure that no one else was listening.

"He didn't dump me, I ran away from the hotel. I'm staying at Carmen Luisa's. Don't worry."

"Why?"

"Mom, Enzo is a very violent person. He beat me with a belt..."

"What? Why don't you come home so we can talk... Or do you want me to go there?"

Maruja hesitated for a moment. "It's not necessary. I'll run some errands and then I'll stop by."

**

The San Judas Tadeo School stood on one

side of the government building in downtown La Neblina. Located in a colonial house, its facade was in perfect condition. Indeed, as a private school, it accepted anyone who could pay the tuition and it served the needs of the children of immigrants from Spain, Germany, Portugal, and Italy.

When Maruja walked in, she spotted Carmen, one of her colleagues. Since she was busy chaperoning a group of children into a classroom, she went directly to the small waiting room to see the headmistress.

"Hello, Maruja. What can I do for you?" the headmistress asked.

"Oh, thank you for seeing me with such short notice..."

"I know you've been calling. I'm sorry I didn't return your calls, but I've been busy," she said, avoiding Maruja's gaze.

"I understand. I was trying to contact you to see if we could arrange my coming back to the school, given the latest developments..."

"Can I get you something to drink? A cup of coffee perhaps?"

"I'm fine, thanks."

"Maruja, I don't think coming back is such a good idea. At least, not right now," she suggested, lowering her head. "Let's wait a while. There's so much turmoil surrounding the issue of your marriage..."

"I don't understand, what does my private life have to do with the fact that I'm a school teacher?" Maruja had a feeling that this conversation was not heading down the right path.

"A lot, I'm afraid. There's a lot of discussion about you running away from your husband, and that affects the reputation of the school. Some parents are saying they don't want you to teach their children."

"I can't go back to my husband, he's dangerous. I need to move on with my life."

"As I said before," the headmistress insisted, ignoring Maruja's last remark, "there are parents who are putting significant pressure on us. Apparently they believe your husband's version of the story."

"Do you?"

"It's not about what I think. We rely on tuitions and donations. You do understand that? If the Italians take their children somewhere else, their support stops. We have to take measures to protect the business."

"Wait a minute, who is calling?" Maruja questioned, jumping out of her seat.

"I'll tell you, but only because I'm worried about you. I don't want any trouble, ok?"

"Enzo?"

The headmistress shook her head.

"Who is it, then?"

"Your mother-in-law," she whispered, her eyes glued to the floor. "She has made significant donations to the school, and asked me personally to not let you set foot in here. She's also calling the teachers. Be careful."

"Concetta?" she pondered aloud in disbelief. "Are you serious? She took over the whole wedding, everything about it, and I know Enzo is her soft spot, but this?"

"Yes, it was Concetta, and it was my impression that she will do everything she can to hurt you."

"How long have I worked for you?" Maruja asked, reddened with anger.

"Don't blame it on me! I know that you're a decent, hardworking person and the children adore you, but I don't hesitate to admit that I'm afraid of Concetta's influence."

"That's great!" Maruja replied. She grabbed her bag and left the office, closing the door carefully behind her.

On her way out, she noticed the empty corridors. "Much better this way, it would be heartbreaking to have to greet them knowing that it might be the last time," she muttered to herself, and rushed out of the building.

Her plan was to walk all the way to her mother's, but then she spotted the brown Dodge Dart taxicab passing by. She hailed it.

**

The cab driver moved slowly through the residential complex and parked in front of house no. 52. The yard was impressive; with well-manicured grass on both sides of the gravel path, and an angel in the fountain held a fish while a stream of water flowed steadily from its mouth.

"It won't take long, would you wait for me?" she asked.

"How long?" The driver looked at her from the rear-view mirror.

"No more than twenty minutes."

"Ok," he replied hesitantly.

Maruja nodded in agreement and left the car. She opened the wrought iron gate, walked past the fountain, and headed to the back, hoping that the kitchen door was open.

"Hello?" Maruja called out.

"What nerve! What are you doing here?" Concetta snapped. She resembled a witch with her curly brown dyed hair and excessive makeup.

"How could you do this to me? You've been spreading lies!"

"That's what happens if you mess around with my boy." She said, moving her hands quickly, her bangles of gold tinkling with every movement.

Money sure don't buy class, Maruja thought. "What did you expect me to do after the beating he gave me?"

"Why are you here? Enzo doesn't want you back." Concetta shifted her attention to some vegetables that needed washing. Something fell from her hands and when she went down on all fours to find it, boasting a massive butt.

"If that what's worrying you, you can sleep like a baby. I don't want him back either. I came because it isn't fair that you're using your influence to destroy me," Maruja tried to reason, looking away from the grotesque picture of Concetta crawling around on the kitchen floor.

"My dear, this is just the beginning. If you hurt my Enzo, you will have to leave La Neblina," she responded matter-of-factly, after retrieving whatever it was that she lost on the floor. "Gino! Gino!" she called.

"What?" a voice responded from another room in the house.

"Hurry up!" Concetta cried, with a slightly hysterical tone to her voice.

Steps approached, and then Gino appeared in the kitchen. He smiled broadly when he saw the intruder. "Hi, Maruja!"

He was about to hug her when his mother interrupted. "Call your dad and tell him that *questa puttana* is here looking for trouble."

"It won't be necessary."

"I told Enzo not to marry you," she said, now peeling a carrot.

"Pity he didn't listen. We all could have been saved the hassle," Maruja said softly.

"A woman with no sense of family, leaving her husband on their very wedding night... Of course, what could you expect from someone who doesn't even know where her real mother is?"

Maruja, who was already on her way out the door, stopped short and turned back, heart galloping.
"Concetta, you are so *sweet*!" Then her voice charged with
irony, "You know what? I wouldn't be surprised if your mom hid from just such a witch as you!"

"What? You've got nothing on my late mother! Out!" said Concetta angrily, her eyes wide open.

Maruja returned to the waiting taxi. One could hear the echo of Concetta's expletives from the kitchen.

**

While she waited for her, Amanda went to Maruja's old bedroom. At the sight of the moving boxes piled up everywhere, she realized that there was so much to pack, but Maruja had insisted on doing it on her return from the honeymoon. Now, everything was so uncertain, she dared to toy with the notion that she might be coming back home for good.

Sitting on the edge of the bed, she looked at all the stuff that Maruja had treasured throughout the years after she had been rescued from the hell she was living in with her biological mother, but that was so long ago... Now she had turned 31, and Amanda didn't want to let her go. On the nightstand, she spotted a compilation of short stories by H. C. Andersen, which she had bought to read bedtime stories from, and which Maruja now used for her children at school.

About that time, she heard the sound of someone in the doorway.

"Maruja! My dear! God bless you. It's so good to see you!" Amanda pulled her daughter into a hug. "Look at you..." she said, through the tears.

"Mom, I'm much better. How are you?" She replied, trying to downplay the whole thing.

"I'm about to go crazy. Why don't you come back to us?" Amanda pleaded with a slight tone of reproach.

"I'm truly sorry, Mom, but I didn't want you to see me like that. Besides, I knew Enzo could come here after me."

"You said that you had some errands to run, did you get them done?" Amanda asked, as she stroked her daughter's hair.

"I went to the school to see if I could start teaching again."

"When will you start?"

"The headmistress wants me to stay away until things calm down." Maruja answered, looking down at her hands. "Concetta is bribing them with her donations to keep me away, but I still believe I can get my job back in time." She wasn't actually sure if she believed it or not, but she tried her best to sound convincing for her mother's sake.

"What if it never happens?"

"What makes you say that?"

"Dear, you are a teacher, and Enzo has destroyed your reputation… I don't want to discourage you, but I don't think any school will be hiring a teacher with your past anytime in the near future."

"Mom, this isn't the Spain you fled from. I have nothing to hide," she replied confidently.

"Yes, but Enzo is saying you're a…" Amanda couldn't finish the phrase.

"Mom, he's saying that because he's afraid of me going to the police."

"Are you going to report him?"

"I love him, but I can't forget what he's done," she said, her eyes still focused downward.

"Is it true what he's saying? Is it true that you've been with other men?"

"I'm appalled at what you're implying. The only man in my life is Enzo," she said with a hint of disappointment in her voice.

"Is it true that you weren't a virgin?"

"It is true," she said. Maruja looked her mom directly in the eyes, as she continued, "But he is the only man I have ever been with."

"What are you going to do?"

"All I know is that I'm not taking him back. Mom, Enzo is sick. He's sweet and caring one second, and the next he transforms into a monster. I won't let him do to me what those men did to my mom, I can't." Tears trickled down her cheek.

"What if he asks for forgiveness?"

"He already did, and I forgave him from the very bottom of my heart, but I won't take him back. Are you
with me on this?"

"You can count on us both, whatever you decide. Maruja, you are the daughter I never had, and Mateo feels the same way."

"Then come with me to the police station. I have to restore my honor."

**

The recent events were affecting Mateo and Amanda as well. Customers disappeared; people who loved to come in and say hello now hurried away or crossed the road to avoid them. They sometimes wished they had left, gone to a new place where everything could be like it was before Enzo came into their lives.

Maruja's situation was in no way better. No job, locked in her room for fear of running into Enzo, people avoiding her on the streets. Everyone seemed to take Enzo's side.

Amanda and Mateo were about to close after a very quiet day, when Salvador walked in the shop.

He was an old friend of Mateo's from Spain, when Franco's dictatorship tightened its grip over the country, sending hundreds of thousands of civilians to prison or exile. Salvador was an active member of the resistance movement, and he did a couple of things that were perhaps better left unmentioned. It was enough to say, his head had a price. Nonetheless, when they crossed the border together, no one paid them much attention, since the police were looking for a single man. Had it not been for Mateo and Amanda allowing him to join them, Salvador would have ended his days in prison or at the hands of the police.

Salvador was indebted, and they had kept in touch all these years. He was there when Amanda and Mateo decided to start the business, a baby shop called "The Golden Stork," and he too regarded Maruja as their daughter when they decided to bring her home with them.

"Compadre!" exclaimed Mateo when he saw his old friend.

"It is so nice to see you. How are you doing?"

"I curse the day Enzo came into our lives!" Mateo answered, lowering his head.

"So I've heard. I came to cheer you up. What can I do for you?"

"No one can mend this, Salvador. Maruja

can't even go out of the house, because people call her names. She lost her job. You should have seen the bruises..."

"No one shops here anymore either..." Amanda added. "Can I get you a cup of coffee?"

"I'd love one," replied Salvador, putting the newspaper he brought with him down on the counter of the shop.

"Interesting news?" Mateo asked, pointing at the newspaper.

"Do you remember Jimmy Hoffa? I didn't know that today, July 30, is exactly one year since his disappearance. 'Still missing: No remains found,'" read Salvador aloud.

"You mean the labor union guy, the one who vanished?"

"Yeah, he was supposed to meet with someone in a restaurant and *vupti*!"

"He never showed up?"

"His wife reported him missing. The police found his car in a parking lot... People disappear, you know?" Salvador said with open arms.

Maruja didn't want to come out, but she couldn't help hearing the last chunk of their conversation.

"You seem mesmerized, Maruja. Why don't you join us? It will cheer you up." Amanda suggested carrying a tray with coffee service.

Maruja jumped when she heard the voice

behind her and then smiled. "Let me help you with that," she said, taking the tray from Amanda and joining the men in the shop.

"Hi Salvador, nice to see you!"

"Maruja, how are you child?" Salvador replied with a shy smile.

"Trying to survive, but by now you must know all about it... How do you like your coffee?" she asked, in an attempt to change the subject.

"Just black, half a cup."

Maruja served the coffee to all of them and then addressed Mateo, who was reading the newspaper. "May I see it when you finish?"

"You can have it now; I only read the headlines..." he replied and handed her the paper.

Snatching the newspaper from him, she walked a couple of steps away from them, avidly reading the front page. She read the full story and then realized that Salvador was about to leave. She approached them and was about to give him the newspaper back, when she suddenly pulled him apart.

"Salvador, may I have a word with you?"

Amanda and Mateo looked at each other puzzled.

**

"Hello?"

"Are you Tomaso Lombardi?"

"Yes, who are you?"

"I've learned that you may be interested in knowing the whereabouts of Cesare Piccio. Is that right?"

"Who is this?"

"That's irrelevant. What matters is the information I have."

"Why should I trust you?"

There was a pause on the line, a slow intake of breath. "Because you want his head as much as I do."

**

"How may I serve you, señorita?" asked the police officer who received them. Maruja and Amanda ignored the sarcasm in his voice.

"I believe that you know perfectly well why I'm here. I came to report my husband."

"You are going to report Enzo Pirozzi?" He smirked, replying with a broad smile, "Sit there."

After what felt like an eternity of waiting, Maruja turned to her mother. "They're just trying to break us. Don't let them get to you."

"Yes, but what if they don't ever come back?" Amanda speculated, annoyed by the treatment they were getting. "They come and go without even looking at us and it is very clear they have nothing else to do. This is ridiculous!"

"Mom, please. We'll gain a lot by filing the report. Just ignore them."

"This is too much! They get coffee, laugh at jokes... Look at that one!" Amanda exclaimed, pointing to an officer sitting with his feet on a desk, while reading the newspaper. "This is outrageous! I'm going home."

"Stay with me, please?"

Just when they were about to give up, the one officer waved at them. He led them into a nearly empty room. The only furniture was a wooden table in the center, four chairs circling it like vultures, and a flickering lamp hanging from the ceiling.

"Before going any further, I warn you that this might lead to nothing. We're low on budget and we have to prioritize. That's the way it is...," he said apologetically.

They sat around the table and the officer beckoned Maruja to speak. From time to time, he jotted a couple of notes on a loose sheet of paper. On occasion, he would interrupt her to clarify a statement or ask a question. When they finished, he called another officer to escort them to the exit. Before even closing the door, he tossed her report in the trashcan.

**

"I need a cup of tea," Amanda exclaimed, heading straight for the kitchen from the front door.

"Me too."

As soon as the kettle whistled that the tea was ready, they sat down around the table, somberly sipping from their cups.

"Do you think they're going to help us?"

"You mean the police? I don't know. At least the report is filed."

Muffled noises came from the living room. Maruja stiffened.

"Did you hear that?"

"Yes, it must be Mateo. Don't worry."

"I'd better go check. Wait for me here."

Maruja tiptoed through the hall connecting the kitchen to the living room.

"You!" cried Enzo, his bloodshot eyes fixed on her. "You reported me to the police!"

"What were you expecting? That I stand forever with my arms crossed?" Maruja replied, feigning a calmness that she was far from feeling. Her heart was about to sprout from her mouth and she could barely hear what he was saying.

Enzo stepped forward and pulled her by the hair. To keep Amanda out of danger, Maruja struggled not to make any noise.

But then, "Maruja, are you going to finish your tea?" she called from the kitchen. "It's getting cold." When she didn't get a reply, she decided to check on her daughter. By the time Amanda got to the living room, Enzo was shaking Maruja by her hair like a rag doll. She ran to help her daughter, but Enzo pushed her away, causing her to stumble and land on all fours.

"You'll withdraw the complaint, even if I have to drag you all the way to the police station myself," Enzo muttered, shoving Maruja out of the house.

"Never! You hear me? Never!" She managed to reply, still struggling to escape from her husband.

"Never?" He stopped short, gasping heavily for a few seconds, and then he punched her on the right eyebrow. Blood splattered across his shirt. He took a piece of cloth from a pile of fresh laundry on the dining room table and wiped Maruja's face. "It's your fault!" He yelled, repressing a sob, "You made me do this!"

"Enzo, I just want my life back!"

"Sorry darling, that would make me look bad," he replied, wiping the blood from his hands onto his pants. "You and your family will have to move away from La Neblina."

He opened the door and paused for a few seconds to look back at the two women. Then, before he could get his wife out the door, a fist caught his jaw and toppled him over.

Enzo tried to get up, but he felt as though he was not in his own body. He reached out to grab something to help regain his balance, but the effort gave him nausea. Everything went blurry. The last thing he saw was two pairs of hands trying to lift him off the ground.

**

"Are you crazy?" Amanda asked her husband and Salvador, who had just dropped Enzo with a single punch.

"Are you really taking his side after all he has done?" Salvador asked, waving at Maruja who was holding the cloth to her eyebrow.

"Dear Amanda, believe me! You don't want to know what I had to do back in Spain...," he said as he pulled Enzo by his legs.

"Salvador, we have enough problems. I don't want him to harm you, too."

"I have a little surprise for this bird. Come on. Help me get this jerk in the car. I promised to deliver him before nightfall!"

"What are you going to do with him?" Amanda asked, trying to stop them.

"He's going to make sure that we all have a future," Maruja replied.

"What future? People call you 'whore' on the streets. You were kicked out of the school where you taught. No one shops in the store anymore; none of us have anything left."

"Maybe not with him around, but I'm sure that he will never, ever bother us again," Mateo reassured her.

"Compadre, are you going to give me a hand or not?" Salvador asked from the doorway.

"I'm coming," cried Mateo, as he turned and ran to help his best friend.

EPILOGUE

Maruja, Amanda, and Mateo were all enjoying a cup of coffee at the Copenhagen airport while they waited for Salvador. It had been three months since they had last seen him in the house in La Neblina.

After Salvador and Mateo left with an unconscious Enzo in the car, Maruja told Amanda everything... "You know what?" Maruja said trembling, "We have to leave the country. Scandinavia is accepting political refugees from Chile."

"Do you have any idea what they're going to do with Enzo?" Amanda asked, sitting next to her.

"I decided to hand him over to an Italian contact. I wasn't his only victim. There's also someone in Italy who wants to make him pay for some past wrongdoings. I really feel like I have to stop Enzo," Maruja explained, as she took Amanda's hands.

"Do you mean that Enzo would probably die?"

"I mean that Enzo has to yield his own fate," Maruja replied in a low voice.

"What's the story about the Chilean passports?"

"We got them from Salvador. He knows

someone from Chile who ran away from Pinochet's henchmen and he happens to be very good at forging documents. Do you remember the last time that Salvador came to visit and you were both so puzzled, because I wanted to talk to him in private? Let's say I got inspired by what I read in the newspaper that day about Jimmy Hoffa's disappearance."

"What if we get in trouble with the Danish authorities?"

"I'm more than willing to take that risk. When we get there, everything will be uncertain. New culture, new language, new life... The question is, do you want to take the leap with me?"

"You are the daughter I never had, of course I'm in," Amanda replied nodding. "I can't believe you were capable of devising something like this..." Amanda continued in amazement. "Why does it have to be us who run away though?"

"I didn't do it alone. Thanks to Mateo and Salvador, all this is possible. I did this because of my childhood and I know that Enzo and Concetta won't leave us alone. It's like they own La Neblina, and I'm just desperate. Do you need more reasons?" Maruja stroked the hair of the woman she considered her mom.

"No, there's reason enough."

"Well then, gather your essentials. There's a contact waiting for us at the consulate of Denmark. Salvador has already made all the arrangements and he will join us there in a few months."

The sound of the doors brought them both back to the present. A group of passengers moved slowly, their attentive eyes scanning in all directions for loved ones who had been waiting for them on this side of the world. The first wave of people scattered, making way for the second. Finally, when there weren't many left, a couple marched slowly, chatting animatedly, through the center of the hall. Maruja instantly recognized her parents' old friend.

Mateo and Amanda jumped up and began to wave.

Salvador said goodbye to the old woman and approached them. They all hugged.

"Plan Hoffa?" Salvador asked.

"Plan Hoffa," repeated Maruja with a cracked voice.

More than one thousand miles from Copenhagen, on the very same day, the mayor of Taormina unveiled an extraordinary Byzantine mosaic depicting the image of the Blessed Virgin Mary with the baby Jesus on her lap. The anonymous benefactor requested that the mosaic be erected in the famous passage of Corso Umberto.

About the Author

Belangela G. Tarazona was born in Caracas, Venezuela, the fourth of five siblings. Born into a family of readers, Belangela discovered her love of books, devouring the works of Gabriel García Marquez, George Eliot, G. Chaucer, Homer, Virgil, Rómulo Gallegos, Tolstoi, M. de Cervantes, Sir Walter Scott, A. Chehov, Mark Twain and Charles Dickens, among many others. She had never known a time that she wasn't reading or dreaming about writing stories.

She is the multi-genre author of The Child of Dawn (nonfiction), Truths of Illusion Series and A Better World (fiction). Having tried her hand as Systems Analyst and Programmer, Freelance Spanish Instructor, QA Assistant and Patent Coordinator, she has come to realize that her true passion is writing.

Belangela was awarded a grant from **"Rieck-Andersens Familiefond"** to translate "The Child of Dawn" into Danish.

Belangela lives (and writes!) in Frederiksberg, Denmark with her husband, and their son.
Visit her on the web at: www.bg-tarazona.net.

www.ingramcontent.com/pod-product-compliance
Lightning Source LLC
Chambersburg PA
CBHW060517030426
42337CB00015B/1926